Dear Ginnie, Ned, Jan and all the Joneses —
To one of the most special families — my love always,

Sherry

10/86

The Executive Memo

The Executive Memo

A Guide to
Persuasive Business Communications

Sherry Sweetnam

JOHN WILEY & SONS

New York   Chichester   Brisbane   Toronto   Singapore

Published by John Wiley & Sons, Inc.
All rights reserved. Published simultaneously in Canada.

Library of Congress Cataloging in Publication Data:

Sweetnam, Sherry.
　The executive memo.

　Bibliography: p.
　1. communication in management.　2. Memorandums.
I. Title.

HF5718.S88　1986　　　　658.4'53　　　　86-7741

ISBN 0-471-81826-7

Printed in the United States of America

10　9　8　7　6　5　4　3　2　1

To Dad, who never quit

Preface

This is not just a book about business writing. It's a book that shows you how to apply the principles of persuasion, salesmanship, and communication to your writing. It is written as a reference book so that you can choose the sections that pertain to your writing needs. Aimed primarily at managers and professionals in large corporations and small businesses, the book shows you how to write so that writing becomes a major tool for marketing yourself. The book contains:

1. Strategies on how to apply communication and persuasion principles to everyday writing problems.
2. Techniques that will help you organize your ideas quickly.
3. Ways to write two to three times faster than you now do.
4. Models of business communications: an information memo, a sales letter, a proposal, a letter of apology, and a "tough-message" memo.
5. Forty-two exercises that reinforce key points, with an answer key, and a full index for reference.

By reading the book carefully, you will be able to rewrite an ineffective memo so it becomes persuasive, interesting, and effective. You will learn how to write with more ease, how to write faster, and how to make your point better so that you can increase your impact at work. You will see tangible results, because this book gives you tangible advice!

This book is not meant as a review of the basics of writing and English. It assumes that you know the basics, that you simply need to review and practice the principles of communications and persuasion.

A few notes on how the book was written:

First, all of the examples are taken from the writing samples of the participants in my communication workshops. The names, dates, and company names have been changed to protect the innocent, the hard working, . . . and the struggling.

Second, I use the word "memo" throughout the book to refer to business letters, memos, reports, proposals, and sales letters. I do this for efficiency and because the principles covered in the book apply to all areas of written business communication.

Third, I make generalizations about writing which, given some situations, may not necessarily work. You must adapt these generalizations to your particular written communication. Without these generalizations the world of writing would seem like an unmanageable subject. Let them be a starting place.

Last, I wrote this book with a word processor. I highly recommend using one if you are serious about developing your writing potential. A word processor helps you write faster and with more confidence. Your writing production will increase enormously. How? The system helps you get over writer's block by letting you sketch out a rough draft and then eliminate what you don't like in one key stroke. Your writing no longer seems so permanent. Surprisingly, too, your fingers can word-process much faster than they can type. And editing is much quicker because of the system's ability to "cut and paste" your ideas. The only drawback is that it takes time to learn how to use a word-processing program. But once you've mastered the technology, you'll wonder how you ever lived without it! Anyone who writes heavily in business should consider acquiring a word processor—it is an essential tool for communicating efficiently and productively.

SHERRY SWEETNAM

New York, New York
February 1986

Acknowledgments

I want to thank everyone who has been so supportive of my work over the past few years. I want to thank my mentor Joe Ross for his encouragement and constant guidance. He always made sure I was moving ahead; without him I wouldn't have had the inspiration to get my ideas published.

Next, I want to thank the people on my staff who have helped Sweetnam Communications develop. In particular, I thank Kay Cuskley for her hard work, Pam Reid for her detailed and accurate work on the exercise sections of the book. Also, thanks go to my good workers—Mei Ching Fung, Ben Kai Bouey, and Jonathan Stone—for helping me run my office smoothly so I could concentrate on the book.

A special thanks to my dear friends and family, who have helped me throughout the years and with this book: in particular, Peter and Blanka Lawson, Jill LeVin, Sue Canfield and Ron Feigal, Alice Hughes, Janet Spratlin, Kathy Kidder, Jim Blew, Mary Russ, and the Dick Doty's in Colorado.

Also, thanks to both my personal and business friends who have helped me learn about the business world and coached me along the way: Janet Gray, Don Mertz, Jean Bubley, and Caela Farren. A special thanks to Linda Pittari for giving me my big break into the business world. And to Woody Rudin.

Above all, thanks to all the people in my workshops. Without them there would be no book. Their eagerness to learn and grow inspired me to continue analyzing business writing and to develop new materials. The material in this book is derived from their concerns, their writing, and their contributions to our group. They are the ones who questioned, and the answers we came up with are the essence of this book.

Thanks to the illustrators Mary Power and John Caldwell for their original artwork, to Nettie Bleich for her active and positive role as my editor, to Kirk Bomont, my patient production supervisor, and to Julie Glass for her outstanding work as my copy editor.

Finally, thanks to my cat, Trinka, who sat on my manuscript and munched off many a page—she's been here by my side the whole way.

S.S.

Contents

☐ **CHAPTER 3**
The Principles of Persuasive Writing   **69**

☐ **CHAPTER 4**
The Voice of Your Writing   **97**

☐ CHAPTER 8
Exercises   175

☐ CHAPTER 9
Resources on Writing   229

The Executive Memo

1

An Overview of Writing

This chapter looks at how our past experiences with writing influence our present attitudes toward writing. It presents a diagnostic checklist to help you identify exactly what your writing needs are and it indicates where in the book to find answers to your questions. The chapter then looks at the differences between effective and ineffective writing, as illustrated in two versions of the same memo—one effective, the other ineffective. Last, it examines the advantages and disadvantages of writing and speaking, to help you make decisions about when to speak and when to write.

☐ OUR ATTITUDES TOWARD WRITING

Many of us in business today write with the same attitudes we held about writing when we were in school. We simply substitute our managers and offices for our teachers and schoolroom. When we confront a blank page, we panic and begin worrying about making our writing perfect. Instead of trusting ourselves and viewing writing as a management or communication tool, we think of our writing as a series of minitests on spelling, punctuation, grammar, and vocabulary. This cartoon illustrates the point:

Writing is learned, it is not a natural ability. Speaking is. We all arrived in this world with the ability to speak. We babbled our way through the first year or two of our lives, inventing our own personal language. By the time we were 2 or 3 years old and had learned the basic grammatical structures and vocabulary of English, speaking had become like breathing to us. We saw no distinction between who we were and what we said. Speaking and being were one and the same.

By the time we reached the age of 4 or 5, we had learned to speak well, because we had learned speech was a powerful tool that gave us control over our lives. Speaking got us what we wanted. When we entered school, however, our lives changed drastically. Teachers gave us new rules about how to behave. We were told:

"Raise your hand if you have something to say."
"Be at school by 8:15."
"Raise your hand if you have to go to the bathroom."
"Line up before you go out to recess."

In first grade we heard an endless string of new rules about reading and writing:

"Read left to right."
"Hold your pencil like this!"
"Write on the line!"
"Use 'i' before 'e' except after 'c'!"
"When you write about yourself, capitalize the word 'I'!"

Then we had another shock! Not only did we have to learn the rules, but we were *rated* on how well we followed them. We were told it was okay to make mistakes and were given erasers. Yet when we spelled creatively, we didn't get A's. We were told that reading and writing were fun. Yet many teachers used writing as a form of punishment. Many of us had to write, "I promise I won't throw an eraser at Johnny again," one hundred times on the board. Reading and writing began to represent a whole system of reward and punishment for us, rather than a source of self-expression, problem solving, entertainment, and fun.

To make it even harder, we were onstage whenever we read or wrote. Our classmates always knew how we stacked up against them. If we stumbled when reading out loud in a reading circle, the "whole world" witnessed our struggle. If we goofed in a spelling bee, everyone knew it.

In the end, school—and writing in particular—became a stage for proving ourselves, and for succeeding or failing academically *and* socially. And so, we learned what we had to do to measure up and to be accepted by teachers and classmates.

In writing, the secret was to produce words, words, words, and more words. Stress was put on the *quantity* of ideas rather than on their *quality*. "Write 276 words on what you did last summer." We learned that filling up the page was often more important than having inspired and creative thoughts. We wrote "in order to" instead of "to," "oftentimes" instead of "often." Early on we learned to beat around the bush rather than get to the point!

In junior and senior high school we diagrammed sentences and memorized the parts of speech. Along the way we met a few teachers who encouraged us to think creatively and to express ourselves in an original way. But for the most part, a lot of our originality of expression was submerged during our years in school, including college.

This scenario of school days may be an exaggeration for some. However, it holds a degree of truth for every person. When you scratch the surface of your own writing attitudes, your reasons for avoiding writing will probably become very clear. For many people, writing means *rules* and being judged.

☐ IDENTIFYING YOUR WRITING NEEDS

Lots of business people think they have a problem with writing when they really don't. The real writing problem at the managerial or professional level stems for the most part from a lack of self-confidence or from a negative attitude toward writing, not from lack of writing skill. In other words, our negative self-judgments hinder our writing, not our language competence.

You can be an effective business writer if you can speak and be understood, *and* if you went through adequate training in reading and writing. After all, writing is based on the spoken word—so if you communicate effectively when you speak, you can communicate effectively when you write.

Some people have the false notion that what business writing is all about is the rules of spelling, punctuation, grammar, and vocabulary. Not so! What writing is all about in business is communicating! It is using those English rules as a means, not an end. Often overconcern for English basics becomes a roadblock and an easy excuse for not writing.

Why Going Back to School Doesn't Make Sense

You may be among those who think that to be able to write effectively they need refreshers in English grammar. But does it make sense to spend hours trying to memorize rules that you will rarely use? There are over one million words in the English language, and over one-hundred thousand rules of grammar. The odds are pretty slim that you can find the magic rules or memorize the words that will serve you best. For myself, I've given up memorizing things I won't use a lot. The reward doesn't justify the time and work.

If you are in doubt about a point of grammar or how to spell a word, why not refer to a good reference book on grammar or to the dictionary? If your English has worked for you so far, why spend anxious hours of your life fretting over the grammar points you may have missed? (You can test yourself on the one area of grammar that is most commonly weak in native English speakers—agreement of subject and verb—by turning to page 192.)

What to Do If You Have a Problem with the Basics

If you think, however, that you need more than just refreshers in English, that you lack essential skills in the rules of English, you must do something about the lack or you'll waste your energy trying to hide your weakness. You might set up a self-study program, buy good reference books, get a tutor, or perhaps take a college course. Many local colleges and universities have grammar hotlines to help answer tricky grammatical questions.

For most business people, however, problems of writing lie less with the basics than with attitude and the organization of ideas.

Self-Diagnosis of Your Writing Needs

The following is a checklist of the areas people are concerned about when it comes to writing effectively. Check the area or areas you want to work on and then refer to the pages in this book that deal with your interests:

_____ Knowing when to write (pages 12–17)

_____ Reviewing the principles of communication (pages 19–67)

_____ Reviewing the principles of persuasion (page 69–95)

_____ Organizing my ideas (pages 50–59)

_____ Getting the spelling, punctuation, and grammar correct (pages 60–62)

☐ EFFECTIVE VERSUS INEFFECTIVE WRITING

The purpose of communication is expression of the human spirit. Communication is a means of expressing what is in our head and our heart. If we could not communicate our spirit to the world, we would feel a profound loneliness and purposelessness. We would be observers in life, rather than participators.

There are three types of communication: speaking, writing, and the nonverbal forms. We are communicating all the time, whether we are speaking or writing or sitting quietly on a park bench. Some experts claim that ninety percent of business communications take place through body language. I will not focus on this aspect of communication in this book, but will list here several ways people express their spirit without talking or writing:

- In their mode of dress
- In the way they spend their time
- In the colors they wear
- By what they do *not* say
- By the environment they choose to live in
- By the plants they buy
- Through the pictures they have in their offices
- By what they read

- By what they watch on TV
- By the work they choose to do
- By their hairstyle

The Rewards of Being an Effective Writer

Communicating effectively in writing means three things: making the point, doing so without unnecessary words, and being persuasive.

The result of being an effective communicator in business is that you help yourself and others to work successfully. If readers know what you expect of them, they can do their job. Also, your being an effective writer helps create trust between you and your readers because they will clearly understand your point of view. People who trust you are more apt to want to work with you or to do business with you. They will *want* to read what you write, to hear what you have to say. They will more willingly be led and managed by you.

The Results of Ineffective Writing

Writing is ineffective when it is unclear, wordy, unorganized, visually unappealing, or when the main points are buried. Here are the results of ineffective writing:

1. Jobs Don't Get Done

Business slows or stops when writing is ineffective. People are not free to act or make a decision because they're confused about what's being said and what they're supposed to do. They have to spend time clarifying information rather than actually doing their work.

2. Time and Money Are Wasted

Ineffective communications waste billions of dollars a year. Think of all the unnecessary hours you've wasted reading and rereading a confusing memo. To clear it up, you had to make a rash of phone calls or take extra trips to someone's office, or you had to attend yet one more meeting. Other people's confusion costs you the most valuable resource you possess: time. And as the adage goes, "time is money."

3. Unnecessary Communications Must Be Written

Fifteen to thirty percent of written business communications are unnecessary. They are simply an attempt to clarify earlier unclear and incomplete communications. If everyone wrote clearly at the start, we could get on with the business of work, rather than the business of trying to figure out what other people mean.

The following examples illustrate how you can turn an ineffective memo (Memo A) into an effective one (Memo B). Notice how Memo B is more effective because it has a plan for each paragraph—(1) purpose, (2) problem, (3) solution, and (4) follow-up.

When you finish reading this book, you will be aware of how to write well-organized and clear memos like Memo B.

MEMO A: Original Ineffective Memo

Subject: Computer Card Procedure

As you know, a new procedure has been recently instituted whereby your unit no longer fills out the old keypunched computer cards for the MIP Commission billings but instead fills out the new computer card generation forms. A clarification of this new process is in order.

Unfortunately, there has been a variety of occasions when Data Entry has been unable to decipher the particular information on those new computer cards that come from your unit. Therefore we must make a specific request that these computer cards be printed more clearly and legibly by your unit personnel and that you use the useful listing that we have prepared for your unit's use. Enclosed you will find a number of copies of company plan listing for the use of anyone in your department who processes the new computer cards.

In addition, it is important to note that your department be certain that each piece of information that is requested on the computer cards be written down in full on these forms. To give you just a few examples: the wire call number, and the account number, etc.

Do not hesitate to contact me if you have any further questions regarding this particular request.

MEMO B: Rewritten Effective Memo

Purpose:
Problem:

Solution:

Subject: Smoother Processing of New Computer Cards

We need your cooperation in the smoother processing of the computer card generation forms for the MIP Commission Plan packages.

Data Entry has been unable to process these forms efficiently for two reasons: (1) the forms have been difficult to read and (2) certain information has been lacking.

Please inform your staff to pay closer attention to the following three items so that the forms can be processed more efficiently:

1. Print more legibly
2. Use the "Company Plan Names" listing (see extra copies attached)
3. Include the following information:
    - wire call number
    - account number

Follow-up:

I will call you on Friday, November 14, to confirm that the processing procedures are working smoothly.

Why Do We Write Ineffectively?

1. We Don't Think Clearly

Clear writing reflects clear thinking. Unless we know exactly what we want to say, we cannot write our ideas clearly on paper. Too often writers meander their way through a memo, never really knowing where they are headed or what they are trying to say. The result is muddy writing. When this happens, readers question whether the writer is too lazy to edit or simply doesn't know how to think clearly.

2. We Write Only from Our Own Point of View

We end up making serious communication errors when we assume our readers have the same point of view that we do. Because of this false assumption we bury or omit information that is critical to our readers' understanding. We may use technical language that is second nature to us but confusing to the reader. We breezily assume that readers will fill in the communication gaps we've left. Instead of doing so, they flounder around, stew over the problem, or phone us for clarification.

It is easy to recognize writing that has a writer-centered technical point of view. We have to work at translating it. Familiar examples are unfriendly computer manuals, IRS tax forms and instructions, and many insurance policies and legal documents.

If you want to express yourself clearly, you must write so that your readers understand from their point of view. They may have an entirely different perspective. If you don't respect their viewpoint, you are writing only for yourself.

3. We Don't Organize Our Thoughts

A major reason for confusing writing is failure to categorize and organize ideas. In fact, each paragraph and sentence should have a distinct theme. A plan is essential for clear writing.

People often think of the word "outline" when they hear the word "plan." In grade school, outlines meant dissecting information into infinitessimal detail and setting up headings, starting with Roman numerals followed by lowercase a's, b's, and c's. That kind of detail is unnecessary in business writing. A basic, simple plan is all that's needed.

4. We Write to Impress

We should write to *express*, not to impress. We think that using big words and long sentences will gain us respect and credibility. In fact, writing to impress causes disconnectedness and miscommunication. How do *you* feel when someone tries to impress you with flowery language? Probably awed or turned off. And often confused. In the end, you don't feel connected to that person; you feel either inferior or superior. You wouldn't like to sit down to lunch, have a beer, or do business with him or her. Flowery language alienates people.

5. We Don't Edit Enough

Because we stop editing sooner than we should, or we don't edit at all, we end up with ineffective memos. We may not know we've been unclear because we have failed to ask for feedback. Or we may honestly not know how to edit to make our writing more effective. Last, we may not edit simply because we want to get the memo off our desk *now*, and be done with it.

How to Tell if Writing Is Ineffective

As readers, we often blame ourselves when we don't understand what we read. We think, "This isn't clear, but it must be *my* problem, because after all this *is* in writing. And I should be able to figure out anything in writing." Because of centuries-old awe and respect for the written word, we blame ourselves for not understanding. In fact, we need to start looking at the written word with a more critical eye instead of automatically blaming ourselves as readers. The following are signs of ineffective writing.

1. **We must go on visual "treasure hunts."** To get the message we are forced to reread, skip around from paragraph to paragraph looking for the main point, or translate what we think the writer is saying into plain English. When we have to ask, "What did I receive this report for?," "I sure can't find any reference as to why I got this," or, "What's the point here???," the writer is forcing us to do the work. What happens? We stop reading and promise ourselves we'll come back to the memo when we have more time. As time passes we keep putting the memo at the bottom of our "to read" pile. If we ever do pick it up later, it's with resistance and resentment.

2. **We get bored.** It is astounding how bored many people are with business reading. Too much of what is read doesn't make sense. The reader has the burden of trying to impart meaning and relevance into the writing.

3. **We feel angry toward the writer.** People damage their business reputations by writing unclearly. Readers feel frustrated, angry, and resentful toward them. "If this guy wastes my time with

his writing, he's probably going to waste my time in person, too. Maybe the problem is he doesn't know how to think clearly. I guess I can't trust him with my business problems."

4. We feel helpless. We are forced into an infantile, helpless state when writing is unclear. *We* are not in control, the *writer* is in charge. He or she has the secret code. Think of how you feel when you have to decipher instructions that have been poorly translated from another language into English. Or when you have to use computer manuals or word-processing programs that omit important steps, deemphasize critical commands, or highlight minor information. (Computer companies now sell rubber hammers so that new buyers can beat up their computers. These hammers testify to the temper tantrums that unclear writing can cause.)

☐ DECIDING WHEN TO WRITE AND WHEN TO SPEAK

Most people, given the choice, would prefer to speak rather than write. Why? Because speaking seems to require less time and seems easier because we've had much more practice at it. Yet at times the most productive, efficient, and appropriate way to communicate is to write.

We need to analyze which form of communication is the most appropriate and efficient for individual situations and to learn to stop avoiding writing if indeed it will enhance our business relationships and achieve our business goals. Here are some critical questions to ask yourself before you decide whether to speak with or write to someone.

- Which form is the more efficient way to communicate?
- Which form is more likely to achieve my business goals?
- Which form would establish the most trust?
- Which form suits the style of the person I want to communicate with? (Does he like shooting from the hip? Does she like time to think about business decisions?)
- How quickly do I need a response?

Before you decide which form to use, you must consider the advantages and disadvantages of each.

Advantages of Speaking

1. Speaking Is Easy. Speaking is easy because we have been practicing all our lives. Probably around 99.99 percent of our communication time has been devoted to it. To avoid the unknown, most people choose to speak.

2. Speaking Is Social, Dynamic, and Alive. Speaking is more fun than writing. We can small-talk, crack jokes, and find out what makes the other person tick. When we're speaking with someone we get immediate feedback. We don't have to wait for a response.

3. We Can Adjust Our Message. There's flexibility and elasticity to speaking. We can instantaneously adjust our message. We can add and delete ideas or speed up or slow down the message, all depending on the listener's reactions.

4. We Don't Have to Worry about Our Words Being "Written in Stone." We feel freer in expressing ourselves in speaking because there's no record of our words. Our message disappears the instant we say it. Therefore we don't have to feel so accountable for every word we speak.

5. It's Easier to Read People When We Speak to Them. There are many communication channels to tune in to when we speak which help us to know our listener better. We have nonverbal cues such as:

- Eye contact
- Facial expression
- Posture
- Tone of voice
- Voice strength
- Business dress

6. Speaking Takes Less Time. We don't have to spend time preparing our communication by drafting words onto paper, getting them typed up, editing them, and then waiting for a response. We can get immediate responses and gratification.

Disadvantages of Speaking

1. We Can Never Verify What Was Said. We can never recapture a conversation or recreate exactly what was said. Our interpretation of what was said is left up to our memories and can never be objectively verified.

2. We Can't Edit Very Well as We Speak. Spoken words often slip out unedited. We sometimes blurt things out we don't mean to say or wish we hadn't said. Once something is said, it can't be erased.

3. We Can Always Deny Having Said Something. Speaking permits us to pass the buck. We can always claim that the other person wasn't listening well and didn't hear us correctly.

4. Speaking Doesn't Make Us Special. Many more people can speak well than can write well. Therefore, speaking ability doesn't necessarily distinguish anyone from the rest of the business crowd.

5. Speaking Isn't Always Time Efficient. Speaking isn't efficient if we have to speak with lots of people, and especially if those people are in different locations. We must take extra time to set up appointments and to travel. Further, speaking requires extra time for social interaction and "schmoozing."

6. Speaking Requires Being Quick on Your Feet. Social business expectations require that a speaker keep pace with the speed and flow of conversation. For a person who likes to take time to absorb information and mull it over before responding, speaking can be a disadvantage.

7. Spoken Words Don't Last. The minute a word is spoken, it's lost forever. Once the speaker is out of the listener's sight, his or her words are soon likely to be out of the listener's mind.

8. Speaking Costs Privacy. There are times when we would rather be alone than with people. When we're with people we must be polite, even when we don't feel like it. We must present our public selves effectively and forgo any present need for privacy.

Advantages of Writing

1. Writing Is a Permanent Record of Thoughts and Events. Writing lasts. It exists in time and space. Writing allows us to have a permanent presence in someone's life even when we're not physically present. Can you imagine the business world existing without the written word? Neither business nor civilization as we know it would exist without writing. Our history and reality would be based on memory, hearsay, and rumors.

2. Writing Forces Clarification of Thought. Wishy-washy memos stem from wishy-washy thinking. To write well, we must know our point of view. The constraints of writing—the paper, the lines on it, the structure of English—all force us to discipline our thoughts.

3. Writing Eliminates Worry. Once we have our ideas written down, we are free to move on to new thoughts and tasks.

4. Writing Forces Action. A written communication has a better chance of being acted on than one that is spoken. A memo won't disappear. It will remain on someone's desk until some action is taken. If we want to get people to deal with us, writing is one of the best ways to do it. Someone can always avoid meeting us in person or talking with us on the phone, but that person will find it hard to ignore our ever-present letter.

5. Writing Gives the Reader Control Over Time. Written communications especially work for people who don't have a lot of time for the social demands of spoken communication. The reader is free to decide when to read and how fast to read. He or she can dive straight into a memo without having to devote extra time to socializing.

6. Writing Makes People Keep Their Word. Writing means making a commitment. When we commit our thoughts to paper, we announce to ourselves and the world our actions and our intentions. Writing keeps us honest.

7. Writing Saves Time and Energy. If we have a message for many people, we can write just one letter to reach them all. Further, we don't have to verbally repeat ourselves—we only have to say it once when we write.

8. Writing Is a Training Tool. Writing is a way of helping people learn. People can read procedural manuals or job descriptions on their own, at their own pace, without the pressure of one-on-one job training. All the how-to books on the market attest to the popularity of writing being used as a training tool.

9. Writing Is a Reference Tool. Can you imagine having to memorize all the phone numbers and addresses of your business associates and friends? Without the written word, our mind and memory would be in "information overload" all the time. Writing serves as a record and is a reference tool, allowing us to move on to other business.

10. Writing Is a Personal Advertisement. Anything we write and make public becomes a public relations piece for us. We get our name seen; we get credit for our ideas.

11. Writing Creates Mental Freedom. Once we make our point in writing, our thoughts on the subject can no longer own us or rule our thinking time. We are free to move on to new horizons.

12. We Have Control Over Our Message. We can write and edit until we produce a communication that says exactly what we want it to say.

13. Writing Buys Time. Writing gives both readers and writers time to figure out a game plan. They feel less pressured to react immediately.

14. Writing Is a Prerequisite for Success. Writing is one of the most highly regarded communication skills in the business world. It can have a lasting influence on people. Writing gives the writer respect, clout, and power. In business, effectual writing is one of the ultimate signs of professionalism and of clear thinking. You cannot succeed in large organizations today without writing effectively. The following illustration says it all.

Disadvantages of Writing

1. Writing Makes Our Words Permanent. In the Latin expression, *scripta manent, verba volant* (writing remains, words fly away). We can't retrieve or change what we've written and made public. The written word cannot be denied, adjusted, or retracted, as can the spoken word.

2. Writing Takes Time. Writing isn't an instantaneous form of communication, like speaking. Drafting and editing a memo usually take longer than does a phone call.

3. The Writer Has Less Control over the Reader's Response. Unless we are experienced and consistently effective writers, we lose some degree of control over how our reader responds to us. We are not present to deal with the reader's questions or objections.

4. Writing Makes Mistakes Permanent. When we fail to communicate effectively in writing, we can't hide it. Our readers know it. Our writing is proof that we have misread the needs of our audience, miscommunicated, or made errors in English.

5. Writing Is Lonely. We are alone when we write. We don't have the fun of social interaction, as we do with speaking; we don't have the outside world to distract us. We are forced to examine our private thoughts alone.

6. Writing Isn't a Live Form of Communication. Writing isn't social and fun and interactive, like speaking is. The written word is the lifeless, fixed form of our lively spoken words and thoughts.

7. Writing Isn't a Natural Skill. We did not come into the world with the skill to write, just as we didn't come into the world with the skill to play the piano or play baseball. These skills are learned and take practice. Writers aren't born; they're self-made and self-taught.

8. Writing Is Hard Work. The ability to write well doesn't come overnight—it takes commitment and lots of practice. Only the individual can decide whether he or she is willing to devote the time needed for this practice. The ultimate questions are whether the rewards of effective writing are enough compensation for the work and whether the skill fits into a lifelong journey toward self-development and self-expression or rather is a "quick fix" for a job requirement.

2

The Principles of Communication

Let's now look at the fundamental principles of communications. These principles apply to both speaking and writing. They comprise the science of communications. They are:

Principle 1. Use your wisdom as a reader.

Principle 2. Clarify your goals.

Principle 3. Be brief.

Principle 4. Be clear.

Principle 5. Be concise.

Principle 6. Be complete.

Principle 7. Organize your ideas.

Principle 8. Be correct.

Principle 9. Make your presentation attractive.

☐ COMMUNICATION PRINCIPLE 1: USE YOUR WISDOM AS A READER

We all possess useful knowledge about how to write without ever picking up a pencil. There's no magic, no secret formula to it. All we have to do is start at the most logical place—with our experiences as readers. Our greatest source of knowledge begins with our personal experiences. Knowing how *we* feel when *we* read business writing gives us powerful ammunition for how to write. What are the two insights we all have as readers of business writing?

Reader Truth 1:
No One Has Time to Read, So Make It Short
Time is a precious resource, particularly in the business world. None of us has enough time in our business day to do everything that needs to be done. Thus we don't want to have to plow through page after page of writing.

Reader Truth 2:
No One Likes Business Reading, So Make It Easy
We often approach business reading with a negative attitude. First, most of us would rather be with people than either reading or writing. If we have to read, we prefer to read what we enjoy—our favorite novels, newspapers, or magazines.

Second, there is too much to read. We feel overwhelmed by the mountains of correspondence in our "in" box. Finally, much of what comes across our desk is written ineffectively. Many memos take up two pages when one page would have been enough. Critical points are buried, and we feel bored and/or frustrated when we read them.

☐ COMMUNICATION PRINCIPLE 2:
CLARIFY YOUR GOALS

One major reason business writing is not usually effective is that writers do not define their goals or purposes for writing. If a writer doesn't know his or her writing goals, the reader certainly can't be expected to know them. Writers who write without knowing their goals expect their readers to take responsibility for giving order and purpose to the writing.

Business writing has three purposes:
1. to inform
2. to persuade
3. to create action.

1. Writing to Inform
The first purpose of business writing is to inform. Examples are:

- Thank-you letters and letters of acknowledgment
- Weekly highlight or status reports
- Compliance reports
- Policy and procedure manuals

Here is a letter that is a clear example of writing to inform. Its purpose was to say "Yes!" to my request for permission to use a memo written by its author, Thomas J. Watson, Jr., former chairman of the executive committee at IBM.

August 15, 1984

Dear Ms. Sweetnam,

I'd be more than happy to have you use the memo on "Gobbledygook" and wouldn't mind having a by-line. It seems to me at the time I wrote it we were getting so doggoned overloaded with special expertise sort of words that ordinary citizens like myself were unable to communicate anymore. So, if you want to use it, by all means do so.

Best regards.

Sincerely,
Thomas J. Watson, Jr.

Reprinted by permission of Thomas J. Watson, Jr. © 1984

2. Writing to Persuade

The second purpose of business writing is to persuade. Examples are:

- Proposals
- Letters of recommendation
- Advertising copy

The following is an example of a business memo whose expressed purpose was to persuade.

PERSUASIVE MEMO

Subject: Purchase of TBS Copy Machine

I recommended we purchase the TBS copy machine for 3 reasons:

1. It has the lowest maintenance requirements of any copy machine on the market.
2. It has $20 ink cartridges that will run a minimum of 5,000 copies per cartridge.
3. It's on sale at a 20% discount price of $1,250.00.

I'd like to speak with you about this purchase at our Friday meeting.

3. Writing to Create Action

The ultimate goal of everyone in business is to create action. We are all looking for results, for change, for ways to make the business run more smoothly, for better working conditions and relationships, and for increased profits. Examples of the types of business correspondence that are written for action are:

- Requests for information or action
- Sales letters

Following is an example of a memo written for action by the head of a branch office of a major financial products firm. Notice how the request for action is direct, precise, and up front.

ACTION MEMO

Subject: Request for Purchase Ideas

As a reminder, please submit to me by 4 PM Friday the following purchase ideas:

- A long-term growth stock
- A tax-exempt bond issue
- A bond trading idea

Thanks.

At some level the writer is always trying to achieve all three purposes just discussed. For example, all written words present information. And they are always meant to persuade the reader that the writer has a valid point of view, that he or she is a clear thinker and an effective communicator. Even if we're not selling a product or service, we are always selling ourselves or trying to persuade others to "buy" our ability to think clearly and communicate effectively.

Some techniques we can use to persuade our readers to believe in our competence as business professionals and effective communicators are:

- Use correct English
- Write clearly and concisely
- Offer sound solutions
- Use appropriate tone and style for the reader
- Select effective words
- Create attractive, easy-to-read layouts

Finally, at some level, we are always trying to create some type of action, either immediate or long term. Even nonaction becomes an action because it involves a thinking process, a decision that "no action is needed" or that "there's no problem here, so I don't have to do anything."

Although in the broad sense our business writing always has the three purposes, we should always write with one specific, immediate goal in mind. In this way we can focus the message and organize our ideas more easily.

Let's see how the three purposes are combined in a concrete example. Let's pretend to write a procedure manual.

On the surface, the sole purpose of a procedure manual would seem to be to inform people how to perform a task; in other words, the writing is an information source. When we look further, however, we can see that the purpose of the writing goes beyond this. It is also meant to persuade. We want to persuade the reader not only to pick up the manual but to continue reading it. The writing also is meant to persuade the reader that we think clearly, know our job, and are effective communicators on paper. In the long run, the writing aims to get people to do their job more effectively, to follow correct procedures. And that is action. If the manual is a smashing success and we get recognition from upper management, then our writing has become our personalized marketing tool and may eventually lead to a promotion—a long-lasting action!

How can you as a writer clarify your goals quickly and clearly? Following are the how-to's.

Strategy 1.   Write Purpose Statements

The best way to clarify writing goals is to write them down. You need to tell both yourself and your readers your reason for writing—if your memo is mainly for information, action, or persuasion. The following are examples of purpose statements.

1. *The purpose of this memo is to update you formally on the status of the scanning process.* (Stated purpose for writing: to inform)
2. *This is to recommend and outline the reasons why we should hire a new secretary for our department.* (Stated purpose for writing: to persuade and to inform)
3. *This is to request your cooperation in making the new mail delivery procedure run smoothly.* (Stated purpose for writing: to request action)

To write purpose statements, all you have to do is write these six magic words: *"The purpose of this memo is"* and then add the purpose. Some variations are:

- *The reason I'm writing is to . . .*
- *This is to . . .* (standard opening for all memos in one major corporation)
- *I'm writing to . . .*

Start including purpose statements not just in your writing but at the beginning of phone conversations and in the meetings you hold. For example, "My reason for phoning is . . . ," or "The purpose of this meeting is . . . ."

I believe that your use of purpose statements will change your life. It will change the way you see the world and the way the world sees you. Here are four reasons why.

1. Purpose Statements Force You to Define Your Writing Objectives

Purpose statements force the issue of what you want to accomplish. They also help you stay on track throughout the paragraphs that follow, because by defining your purpose you've decided where you're headed.

2. Purpose Statements Gain You Respect from Your Readers

Purpose statements demonstrate that you live with intention and direction. When you tell readers that you have a plan and are clear about that plan, readers pay attention.

3. Purpose Statements Eliminate the Need for Double Reading

By giving your readers clear statements about why you're writing, you give them a clear picture on *how* to read your memo and *what* to look for.

4. Purpose Statements Create Action Faster

Your statement puts readers at ease; they can read with a positive attitude rather than with resistance and frustration. If you point out in the first paragraph that an action is needed, your memo will probably be read immediately or at least placed at the top of the "to read" or "to do" pile.

Strategy 2.   Place Purpose Statements Up Front

When you place a purpose statement in the first paragraph, your readers know from the beginning why you are writing. They don't have to go on a treasure hunt. Too often purpose statements are buried. Here is an example of a buried purpose statement.

DICKSTEIN, SHAPIRO & MORIN

ARE PLEASED TO ANNOUNCE THAT

HELEN R. KANOVSKY

FORMERLY SPECIAL ASSISTANT TO THE SECRETARY,

EXECUTIVE ASSISTANT TO THE UNDER SECRETARY

AND ASSOCIATE EXECUTIVE SECRETARY,

DEPARTMENT OF HEALTH AND HUMAN SERVICES

AND PREVIOUSLY

SPECIAL ASSISTANT TO THE SECRETARY,

DEPARTMENT OF HOUSING AND URBAN DEVELOPMENT

HAS RETURNED TO THE FIRM

2101 L STREET, N. W.
WASHINGTON, D. C. 20037

598 MADISON AVENUE
NEW YORK, N. Y. 10022

FEBRUARY 1, 1981

Why not just say, "Helen's back"? It took the writer too many words to get to the purpose, the important news. If the purpose here was to tell the latest news *and* to impress, neither goal was achieved. As readers, we're turned off and lose interest when the writer runs on and on and delays the purpose.

The following is another example of a buried purpose statement. Notice how much clearer the rewrite is.

Buried Purpose Statement

After Mr. Ari raised certain issues regarding our earlier proposal for Retail Bank training, which was approved by the Retail Bank, the Training and Development Department completed a comprehensive review of that proposal.

Up-Front Purpose Statement

This report is a comprehensive review of the proposal for the Retail Bank Training Program. The original proposal was approved by the Retail Bank. Subsequent to that approval, Mr. Ari raised certain issues regarding the proposal.

Six Common Questions about Purpose Statements

1. When Can You Always Use a Purpose Statement?

Very simply, *to get started*. The words "the purpose of" will always help you get your pencil moving across the page. If you like, you can rephrase or edit out the purpose statement later.

The important thing is that you never have to worry about your first six words in a memo, letter, report, or proposal. These words can be standard, just like the "starters" you used during your school days—your name, the date, and your homeroom number.

2. Can a Memo Have More than One Purpose?

Yes! Most of our memos are multipurposeful: to inform, to persuade, to create action.

3. Can You State the Purpose in Both Subject Title and First Paragraph?

In general, I say yes! The subject title and opening sentence serve two different functions. In the title the purpose serves as an attention grabber. In the opening paragraph the purpose is a more developed and detailed communication and serves as a natural lead-in or "hello" for the whole memo.

The following example shows how the purpose can be stated in both the subject title and the opening sentence without sounding repetitious.

Subject: Request for Approval on Purchase of XYZ Personal Computer

The purpose of this memo is to request that you approve the purchase of an XYZ personal computer by mid May. There are three reasons why this purchase is necessary. First, . . .

The acid test for effectiveness is to actually try writing your purpose statements in the subject title and opening paragraph. If it sounds repetitive, eliminate one.

4. Won't Constant Use of the Opening, "The purpose of this memo is," Make It Just Another Overused Phrase?

This is a legitimate concern. The phrase hasn't yet become standard procedure in the business-writing world. The key is to vary the phrase sometimes or to omit it entirely and just get to the point immediately. For example, instead of writing, "The purpose of this memo is to recommend x, y, z," you could write, "I recommend x, y, z."

5. Which Is Best—a General or Specific Purpose Statement?

It depends on how direct you want to be. You must decide what's appropriate to each situation. The following are two purpose statements, one very general to avoid coming on too strong, and the other very specific because the goal is to get right to the point.

General Purpose Statement

This is to request your cooperation in helping to run a smoother vault procedure.

Specific Purpose Statement

This is to request that you lock the vault door every evening at 5:30 p.m.

6. When Are Purpose Statements Unnecessary?

Clearly purpose statements are not needed in the following three situations:

- **For Routine Communications.** If you write the same type of memo on a regular basis, your readers will already know its purpose. For example, a weekly status report probably wouldn't require a purpose statement.
- **In Some Selling Situations.** If you are trying to sell something to a reader who isn't interested in buying, easing into the sale makes more sense. We'd be laughed at if we wrote, "The purpose of writing you is to sell our consulting services to you." The sale of products and services requires more subtlety.
- **When You Have to Say "No."** If you have to deliver a "tough message," easing into the "no" works better than stating it in the first paragraph. An up-front "no" is a slap in the face. How would you react if, after working hard on a proposal, your client wrote the opening sentence, "The purpose of this letter is to tell you we will not use your proposal"?

☐ COMMUNICATION PRINCIPLE 3:
BE BRIEF

We have a natural prejudice against long memos. Short memos win because they take less time to read. Suppose you had the choice of reading two memos on the same subject, one of them a one-page executive summary and the other three pages of basically the same information. You would automatically choose the shorter of the two because it would require less of your time.

Strategy 1.   Strive for the One-Page Policy

For most business people, anything longer than one page seems too long to read. One manager at IBM says she *refuses* to read anything over one page long. She feels that if the writer can't express it in one page, he or she doesn't have a clear idea. A general guideline thus is, "Make it one page!"

The one-page policy may be impossible in your situation, but it should serve as a goal. This policy is especially appropriate for sales letters. Many headhunters say that resumes shouldn't be longer than one page.

What happens if your memo is not brief? You run a high risk of not being read. However, the real issue is not the length of the memo but the quality of the writing. Most readers stop reading *not* because a memo is two or three pages long but because the memo is written ineffectively. A piece that is concise, clear, and persuasive *and* three pages long has nothing that will hinder someone from reading it. A memo that is well written is fast and effortless reading. By the same token, a short and meandering one-page memo can call for a double or triple reading, and thus the same amount of time needed to read an effective three-page memo!

The key to enticing readers into reading a long memo is to grab their interest in the first fifty words—or in the subject title and first paragraph. If you can do that *and* the writing continues to be effective, you'll hook them. They'll forget about the length and will read on. The hitch with long memos is getting readers over their initial prejudice against anything longer than one page.

What happens if you write a long but effective memo and it still doesn't get read? You must analyze where the problem lies. If you critique yourself and decide that you did indeed write effectively, then the problem is that the reader couldn't get over his or her initial prejudice against long memos. Recognize that this is your reader's perception problem, not your writing problem.

If you suspect your memos are not getting read, check their length. You know you don't like to read lengthy memos, so try to cut the length of your own.

☐ COMMUNICATION PRINCIPLE 4: BE CLEAR

Clarity is the single most critical ingredient in being an effective communicator. In one survey, business executives were asked to analyze the written communication skills of their corporate managers. Ninety-one percent of them said that clarity was the single most serious problem in business writing.

What is clarity? It is the creation in the reader's mind of the same picture the writer has in his or her mind. The writer says exactly what he or she means and there is no room for misinterpretation.

A Reading Standard for Clear Writing

A person who reads only at a sixth-grade level should be able to understand your writing, regardless of the subject matter or its technical or political complexities. Some business people like to believe that their business is so complex that only those in their industry or their profession can understand it. In fact, communicating effectively means demystifying complex issues so that readers can easily understand them.

What Are the Results of Unclear Writing?

When writing is unclear, people misinterpret what is meant. Different readers can read the same memo and then perform the task it outlines in different ways. Ultimately, communication errors mean that jobs don't get done correctly or on time. When writing is unclear, we as readers have difficulty picturing what the writer is trying to say. Our eyes skip around in our effort to make sense of the words. The following are samples of unclear writing taken from a business report and a proposal.

Example 1

The overall plan while definitely showing a need for a Special Services Department within Marketing falls short on producing an accurate statement to the extent in which the Operations Division would be impacted by the development of the Special Client Program.

Example 2

Since efficient marketing depends on the amount of data available through systematic observation, this report will be based on understanding the marketing process, following the marketing methodology given in the seminar through an empirical format substantiated by some assumed information regardless of the credibility of the assumptions made.

Unclear communication is sometimes a business tactic. Some writers use vague, unclear writing to stall for time or to deceive intentionally. A lawyer friend told me that at times he and his colleagues are compelled to write wordy, vague letters so that they can gain time and throw off the opposition.

How to Check for Clarity

1. Conduct the "TV Show" Test

Start giving the TV Show Test to everything you read (or hear in conversation). Decide whether you have a clear visual image of what the writer is saying (as you would watching a movie or a TV screen) or whether you have an unclear picture ("static").

If you experience static, the writer isn't being clear and must do some rewriting.

2. Conduct the "HWIST" Test

HWIST means "How would I say this?" Often when our pencil does not get it right, our tongue will. The process to go through is to think to yourself, "How would I say this?" and then speak your thoughts outloud. Then immediately write it down exactly as you just said it.

Strategies for Being Clear

1. Be Explicit

Spell out in the clearest of terms exactly what you mean to say. Don't make the reader guess. Write so that you leave no room for misunderstanding. Here's an example of a sign begging for misinterpretation.

"MAYBE THE SIGN ISN'T EXPLICIT ENOUGH?"

Source: Writer's Digest. *Reprinted by permission of Schochet.*

On the other hand, some signs are explicit and leave no room for misinterpretation (these are from the New York City area):

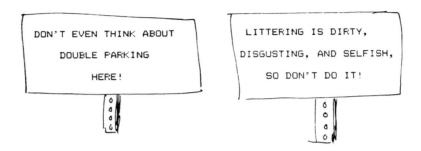

2. Use Short Sentences

We tend to overuse long sentences as a result of our writing experiences in school. Long sentences tend to be complicated and difficult to read. Try using shorter sentences. They are clearer and more dynamic and decisive. This doesn't mean you can't use long sentences; sentence length *should* be varied to some degree so that your writing has a good rhythm. But remember, when you write long sentences that have two or three ideas in them, the reader may have difficulty figuring out what the main idea is and what the relationship is between the ideas. Try not to let any sentence exceed three typewritten lines.

Stick to the rule: *Each sentence should contain one idea.* This forces you to clarify your thinking and to break each idea down into a manageable, identifiable unit. Once you consciously use short sentences, you can if you choose go back and combine two such sentences into one longer one.

One way to test for comfortable sentence length is to read your sentences out loud. Check for flow and naturalness, and compare what you have written with how you would say it. If you have to use more than one breath per sentence and "come up for air" repeatedly, your sentences are too long.

3. Be Specific

When you use specific words, concepts, and numbers, your readers will have a clear idea of what you're saying. For example:

Use specific numbers. Avoid vagueness by using exact numbers with times, dates, prices, percentages, and so on.

Vague	Specific
Almost all	Eighty-nine percent
Volume was up	Volume reached just over 100 million shares a day

Use specific words. Whenever you see the following words, be wary; they are vague and need further development.

assistance	matter
attention	problem
difficulty	please advise
help	situation
issue	subject

Develop and expand on very general words such as "problem" and "assistance." For example:

General	Specific
We have a *problem*.	We are having a problem with late deliveries.
Thank you for your *assistance*.	Thank you for your assistance in speeding up the delivery procedure.

If you feel that being clear is something you need to work on, read the following poem and remind yourself of the power of writing in clear, plain English.

Keep It Simple

Strike three.
Get your hand off my knee.
You're overdrawn.
Your horse won.
Yes.
No.
You have the account.
Walk.
Don't walk.
Mother's dead.
Basic events
require simple language.
Idiosyncratically euphuistic
eccentricities are the
promulgators of
triturable obfuscation.
What did you do last night?
Enter into a meaningful
romantic involvement
or
fall in love?
What did you have for
breakfast this morning?
The upper part of a hog's
hind leg with two oval
bodies encased in a shell
laid by a female bird
or
ham and eggs?
David Belasco, the great
American theatrical producer,
once said, "If you can't
write your idea on the
back of my calling
card,
you don't have a clear idea."

Reprinted by permission of United Techologies. © 1985 United Technologies.

☐ COMMUNICATION PRINCIPLE 5: BE CONCISE

The standard definition of "concise" is "using no unnecessary words." Often we use two or three words where just one will do. In fact, most writers could cut down their writing by at least one third. That third constitutes both unnecessary language and unnecessary information. As my writer friend says, "Write it down first, and then go back and give 30 percent of your words to Goodwill." Wordy writers end up being wish-washy writers: Their writing lacks confidence, directness, or decisiveness.

An example of using too many words, of not being concise, of being long winded, wordy, verbose, airy, not to the point, overdone (getting bored? feeling tired?) is . . . the very sentence I am now writing. Notice your reactions to a message written in both a wordy and a concise fashion:

Wordy: To assist us in this regard, we would appreciate it if you would kindly insert . . .

Concise: Please insert . . .

The first phrase is, as Shakespeare would say, "much ado about nothing": Fifteen words are used to say the same thing that two words say just as well.

Some people get confused about the difference between being concise and being brief. To be brief means to be short—one page short, if possible. To be concise means to use just enough words to make the point. Being concise has nothing to do with whether the length is short or long. For example, a five-hundred-page report that has no unnecessary words would be considered concise. And a half-page memo could be wordy, because it's filled with repetitious ideas, and hollow, empty language.

Why Are We Wordy?

1. We Learned to Be Wordy in School

Writing with lots of unnecessary words is the way we wrote in school. That's one tactic we used to earn us A's. Instead of writing "often" we wrote "oftentimes," instead of "to" we wrote "in order to." Without thinking we continue that wordy style in business.

2. We Think that Using Lots of Words Appears Professional

Many people have the misconception that the more words they use, the more professional and important they appear. With every word and comma, they feel as though they're earning their way up the rungs of management and being a professional.

3. We Think that the More Words We Use, the More Valuable We Are

Written words are measurable, living proof that we are doing something important. Every word is a product that we've manufactured. With each word, we can say, "See, I'm producing, I'm doing my job!"

4. We Fear that Our Readers Will Think We Have Nothing Important to Say

When we're insecure, we say too much. We are afraid that if we don't fill up the page, our readers will think we haven't said anything important. This fear of the empty page is similar to our fear of silence and quiet. We like to fill up large, emptyrooms with things, too-quiet places with people, or silences in conversations with talk. We want objects and words around us because they are a sign of our existence and worth.

One solution to the problem of a very short memo is to center the words on the page and to use wide margins, so the page doesn't seem so empty.

5. We Don't Take the Time to Edit

People are often aware that their writing could be more concise but they prefer to work on other business. Doing that one last edit doesn't get the priority it should.

6. Our Cultural Heritage Says More Is Better

Most of us have two or three cars, two or three color TVs, closets filled with unworn clothes, and basements filled with garage-sale junk. Just as we buy things that we don't need, we use words we don't need.

7. We Believe that the "Company Style" Is Wordy

Some writers believe that their managers *expect* them to fill up the page no matter how short their message. The need to write with unnecessary verbosity is one of the big myths of business culture. The myth continues because of what we learned about writing in school and because of lack of general awareness about what makes a written communication effective.

Why Do Some People Write Too Concisely?

Some writers write *too* concisely. They misinterpret "be concise" as meaning, "be short." Unfortunately, when they are so "short and sweet" they may be incomplete in information or abrupt in tone.

If you are too concise, you end up sounding like a robot on paper. Your written voice sounds curt and rude, and the rhythm of your language becomes staccato and unnatural. Hacking away too many words cuts into diplomatic phrasing and eliminates the trust words that provide a naturalness to the written voice. In essence, you're cutting out the meat along with the fat.

Some people believe that cutting down on volume is the one "big answer" for effective writing. This appears to be a fast and easy editing technique: just cross out unnecessary words. They believe that if they concentrate on being brief, their writing will be effective. They know that being concise is critical, since they observe excellent managers speaking and writing without unnecessary words. But in the effort to be concise, they leave readers confused, because they have left out the key words that communicate an idea or an important attitude.

Being concise is far more than just crossing out unnecessary words. It's making decisions about what words are necessary: what to include as well as what to throw away. In fact, being concise is one of several equally important writing principles. All of them must work together: clarity, completeness of message, conciseness, organization, and persuasiveness.

Strategies for Being Concise

Following are four strategies for being concise.

1. Avoid Redundancy
Don't repeat words that mean the same thing. For example:

Wordy	Concise
a written letter	a letter
maintain ongoing	maintain
right and proper	right *or* proper (not both)

2. Shorten Wordy Phrases
Here are examples of how you might use three unnecessary words where just one will do.

Wordy	Concise
at this time	now
as soon as	when
inasmuch as	since
in view of the fact that	because
in order to	to

3. Avoid "It" and "There" Expressions
Use of the words "it" and "there" at the beginning of sentences often signals false starts and weak beginnings. "It" sometimes signals a phrase or group of words that is of minor importance to the major

point of the sentence. "It" and "there" cannot always be avoided in writing, but try to minimize their use. You will be forced to use more powerful verbs and will get to the point faster.

Some examples of common "it" phrases to avoid:

- It has come to my attention that . . .
- It is necessary that . . .
- It should be noted that . . .
- It is evident that . . .
- It will be important to . . .

Here are examples of how you can change vague "it" phrases to more powerful statements.

Original:	It is interesting to note that ABC Company's profits were up 20 percent last quarter.
More Effective:	Notice that ABC Company's profits were up 20 percent last quarter.
Original:	It has been brought to my attention that the copy machines need new cartridges.
More Effective:	The copy machines need new cartridges. or Bob Barton informed me that the copy machines need new cartridges.

4. When You Have Lots of Numbers, Put Them in Columns

A common tendency of writers is to include lists of numbers in sentences. The words then outweigh the numbers and the impact of the numbers is diminished. When many percentages, price quotes, or other statistics are mixed in with words, we cannot easily digest the significance of the numbers or remember them. It is also hard to refer back to them—we must reread all the words to locate the key numbers.

Following is an example of the same information, first written with lots of words and then written in columns and headings. Notice how the second is faster to read and the information easier to grasp. (And the second is twelve words shorter.)

Original: **Buried Numbers**

An analysis of the costs for external programs shows two significant cost categories. For programs lasting six weeks or less, the average tuition is $4,025, with a range of $2,500 to $4,800. For programs lasting nine weeks or more, the cost rises to an average $9,706. The most expensive is $13,750; the least expensive is $4,700.

Rewrite: **Numbers in Columns**

An analysis of the costs for external programs shows two significant cost categories:

Programs	Average Tuition	Tuition Range
6 weeks or less	$4,025	$2,500–$4,800
9 weeks or more	$9,706	$4,700–13,750

If you feel that you need to work on being concise, read this poem and try to remember its main idea: that some of humankind's thoughts have been expressed in very few words.

Memo To Those Who Write Memos:

Art Buchwald tells of the kid who visited his father's office. When asked what his father did, the kid said, "He sends pieces of paper to other people and other people send papers to him." When you draft a memo, remember other people love to "correct" drafts. The more textually taut you keep it, the less chance for others to pounce on it. The Lord's Prayer has 71 words. The Ten Commandments have 297. The Gettysburg Address has 271. The legal marriage vow has two. General McAuliffe at the Bulge made his point in one: "Nuts!" For practice, send your memo to yourself as a straight telegram at your own expense. Chances are, the less your telegram costs, the more effective your memo is.

Reprinted by permission of United Technologies. © 1985 United Technologies.

☐ COMMUNICATION PRINCIPLE 6:
BE COMPLETE

To be complete means to use the right amount of detail. The common tendency is to give too much information or too little—to undercommunicate or overcommunicate.

How much is the right amount of detail? Asking someone else to tell you what details to include in your writing can be compared with a nuclear scientist asking an outsider what to include in a report on nuclear fission. The scientist is the one with the technical expertise. No one else can tell him or her what information to include or exclude. The same goes for you and your work. What to include is a matter of personal judgment.

How do you know if you've used too many words? First, put yourself in the position of the reader. Try to compare the situation with how you feel after you've had a meal. Reading something that has the right amount of words is like eating the right amount of food. You have just enough. Reading something that has too many words and gives unnecessary information is like stuffing yourself with a ten-course dinner. You're so full, the meal is a blur. On the other hand, reading something that is too concise, too "bare bones," is like leaving the table still hungry. You are left with a sense of incompleteness, of "Is that all there is? There should be something more!"

In other words, you will know instinctively if you have used the right amount of words. Your writing will have the right "feel" to it, from the angle of both the reader and the writer. If you are not complete, you will feel uncertain.

You may react negatively to this idea of knowing by instinct, because you don't know *how* this will come about. People want to know "how to" do something, not what it's supposed to *feel* like. However, you'll find that if you pay attention to your writing, if you'll "know" it has the right amount of words or not. First write, then react.

Looking at an unedited page filled with your words is like looking at the ice cream choices at "31 Flavors." You have to make decisions.

If you know what you want, no problem. If you don't, deciding is difficult. In writing, making choices is even more difficult, especially when the stakes are high.

Why do people have a problem deciding on the right amount of detail? People overcommunicate or undercommunicate either because they are not familiar with the subject and therefore aren't sure what is important (a common problem for people in a new job) or because they don't know their reader's needs. Understanding the reader's needs is particularly tricky when there are multiple readers and each comes to the page with different interests and knowledge.

What Is Overcommunication?

Overcommunication is use of too much detail. I call it the "shotgun approach" to writing because it overloads the reader with unnecessary information. The following is an example. These instructions were on the back of a breakfast cereal box:

1. *Open top of box; remove sack of cereal. Snip open one corner; pour out amount needed. Fold sack to reseal; replace in box. Store in dry, cool place.*
2. *Slowly stir . . .*

Here's another example of overcommunicating. This sounds chatty, almost as if it were dictated.

> *I happened to see Jodi Herron only yesterday, and I was pleased to learn from her that just last Thursday, on September 21, our best supervisor, Amy Levin, got a promotion.*

Why didn't this writer just say:

> *Jodi Herron promoted Amy Levin on September 21.*

People also overcommunicate when they are writing for themselves, not for their readers. They end up "blowing their own horn" or writing CYA (cover your a__) paragraphs and memos rather than getting down to business. Lots of extra words are spent on the victories of departments and people rather than on solutions to business problems. Getting recognition by means of writing makes sense, but not when the purpose of the writing task is to solve a problem.

What Happens If You Overcommunicate?

1. You Waste Time and Money
Unnecessary writing takes up extra time: writing time, typing time, and reading time. Time is money. It also wastes paper and copying resources.

2. You Run the Risk of Not Getting Read
No matter how interesting the subject or how great the monetary reward you may be offering, if you write something that has too many details, you run the risk of not getting read. In the fall of 1984 a well-known magazine ran one of its annual sweepstakes for a million dollars. Several people in my workshops complained about the long and laborious instructions—page after page of fine print; roundabout, wordy writing. Because the directions were too detailed, potential contestants threw their entry cards away. Not even the possibility of winning a million dollars was enticing enough to lure these readers into tackling the labyrinthine instructions.

How to Avoid Overcommunicating

1. Use Headings
When you have multiple readers with varied interests and knowledge, I recommend that you use headings. Each reader can then pick and choose what to read. *The New York Times* organizes articles this way. Readers can easily skip over the details they don't need.

2. Give the "So What?" Test
Reread your writing from the point of view of the reader. Look for ideas and information that make you say, "so what?"—and then give those words and ideas to Goodwill.

Undercommunicating—or the "Bare Bones" Writing Syndrome

The flip side of overcommunicating is undercommunicating—including too little detail or not enough critical information. When we undercommunicate, readers are left with unanswered questions. They can conclude either that we don't care about the memo because we didn't take the time to make it complete, or that we don't understand what information is critical to readers. When we leave out critical information, we are writing from our point of view, not from our readers'. Undercommunicating forces readers to make additional phone calls or set up extra meetings to get their unanswered questions answered.

Why Do People Undercommunicate?

1. They Want to Avoid Writing

They interpret the words "be concise" and "be brief" as "You don't have to write much." When asked what effective writing is all about, they say that it is "concise . . . brief . . . short and sweet . . . to the point." Or they'll talk about using the "KISS" method (Keep It Simple, Stupid). This philosophy justifies their dashing off a quick and underdeveloped memo.

2. They Are Experiencing Writer's Block

Some undercommunicate because they are tongue-tied on paper. This happens particularly with a high-risk memo. They either don't know what they want to say and how to say it, or they can't transfer their thoughts from their head to the paper.

The Complete Written Communication

For a memo to be complete, it must have the same components as any spoken communication. We unconsciously organize our conversations into three sections. Our writing needs to have the same three divisions:

Conversation	Memo
Hello	Introduction
Blah, blah, blah	Body of the memo
Good-bye	Closing

Omission of any of these sections will make the writing seem off-balance or incomplete. The most common omission is the closing—either writers can't think of what to say or they forget to close. (See pages 113–114 for information on how to close.)

☐ COMMUNICATION PRINCIPLE 7:
   ORGANIZE YOUR IDEAS

Your ideas should be organized throughout your memo. Each sentence and paragraph should flow logically from the one before. Organization should work for the entire communication, at the sentence level, the paragraph level, and the whole memo level.

How to Organize a Paragraph

The paragraph is the unit we use to group similar thoughts. Each paragraph deals with one thought or theme. As the paragraph progresses, the core thought is logically developed and elaborated on by supporting details and documentation.

To test for effective paragraphs, try to identify the purpose of each paragraph, or the question that each paragraph provokes. In your next-to-last draft, write these in the margin alongside the text, and then make sure there is a logical flow from one idea to the next.

The business paragraph has two elements: the lead sentence and the body.

1. The lead sentence. The lead sentence opens the paragraph and summarizes its main idea. In school we used to call the lead sentence the "topic sentence." I recommend short lead sentences because they have more punch than long ones.

2. The body of the paragraph. The body of the paragraph expands on the ideas in the lead sentence. Here the writer develops the main theme and gives details to support it.

The following paragraph is a good example of a lead sentence and body. Notice how the lead sentence prepares the reader for what's to come, and how it is directly supported by information in the body.

lead sentence

> We have two different services that offer the small investor a discount. One of these, our Sharebuilder Plan, offers a rate that would be less than half that charged for a regular transaction. The other, Individual Discount Service, provides a 15 percent discount from the regular rates.

How to Organize a Memo

You must have a plan for everything you write. Without one, you won't be clear. The following models show how to organize whole memos and what information to give in each paragraph. First the original memo is given, and then a rewritten version, to demonstrate how much more effective the organized memo is. Notice that in the rewrite, each paragraph has *one theme.*

Whether you start from these step-by-step models or just write and write, ninety-nine percent of the time you will end up with the same structure anyway. The models can serve as a starting point for your writing. Included are:

- An information memo
- A letter of apology
- A procedure memo
- A proposal

1. Model for an Information Memo

Use the following 4-point organizational model if your critical purpose is to inform or to solve a problem:

```
1.  Purpose
2.  Problem
3.  Solution
4.  Follow-up
```

Notice how in the original memo the purpose of each paragraph is unclear. In the rewrite, each paragraph has one purpose: to state the purpose, problem, solution, and follow-up.

MEMO A: Original Memo

Subject: ADS Secretarial Password

Effective April 1, 1986, secretaries will no longer be assigned passwords to access their principals' Audio Distribution System calls. Secretaries will still have the capability of receiving the names of the called parties by simply depressing the "#" key on their touch-tone telephones.

Once the "#" key is depressed, the system will respond, "New message from (name of party calling)." After the secretary writes down the name, she can hang up.

This procedure is being put in place at this time for easier secretarial coverage of ADS calls. Please inform your managers of this procedure immediately.

If you have any questions, please contact Bonnie Hiller on 4-555-1313.

MEMO B: Rewritten Memo

Purpose:

Problem:

Solution:

follow-up:

Subject: New Procedure for ADS Calls

The purpose of this memo is to inform you of the new procedure designed for easier secretarial coverage of ADS calls. Please inform your managers that this procedure is effective April 1, 1986.

The old procedure created extra steps. Now secretaries will no longer need to use passwords to access their principals' Audio Distribution System calls. They simply have to depress the "#" key on the touch-tone phones to receive the name of the calling party.

Steps of the new procedure:

1. Depress "#" key.
2. Listen for system response:
   "New message from (name of party calling)."
3. Write down the name.
4. Hang up.

Thank you for seeing that the ADS procedure is followed. Please contact Bonnie Hiller on 4-555-1313 if you have any questions.

2. Model for a Letter of Apology

The major goal of any business is to keep customers happy. If customers aren't happy, the business fails. Here are some interesting facts about unhappy customers:

- On the average, a customer who has had an unpleasant experience with a business will tell *nine to ten* other people.
- Fifty-four to seventy percent of these complainers can be won back if you resolve their complaints.
- Ninety-five percent will become loyal customers if their complaints are handled *well* and *quickly*.*

If a customer of yours has a complaint, you must get it resolved as quickly and as satisfactorily as possible. Writing a letter of apology is

*From *Customers Mean Business,* Direct Selling Education Foundation, 1982.

one of the best ways to do this. The following is a possible order for the letter of apology.

---

1. **Reference message:**
   - Refer to the account.
   - Refer to previous communication.
   - Refer to the history of the problem.

2. **Good news message:**
   - Say that action has been taken.

3. **Apology/empathy statement:**
   - Use the word "apology."
   - Use the words "I'm sure you felt. . . ."

4. **Documentation statement:**
   - Explain the action that has been taken.
   - Document the problem (action, date, time, names).

5. **Goodwill message:**
   - State the customer's value.
   - Stress the continued relationship.

The number one priority when you're writing a letter of apology is: *Don't bury your apology.* Think about your own expectations for how you want to be treated. If a friend of yours promises to meet you at a restaurant at 6:30 and shows up at 7:00, the first thing you expect is an apology. Up front. Until you get one, you will not be completely open to listening to your friend. Once you get your apology, you can begin to have a good time.

In my experience, strong managers apologize up front and then swiftly move on to the business at hand. This is an honest, direct, and sincere approach to communications. The following is an example of a revised letter of apology.

MEMO A: Original Memo

Dear Mrs. Cuskley,

In response to your letter of July 11, the following actions have been taken:

1. We have credited your account $0.83 to adjust the incorrect margin charge in May.
2. Since the $1302 was not actually invested in Ready Assets until 6/9/85, we have credited interest from 2/2/85 to 6/9/85. According to our money funds system, the adjustment amount is $36.33, representing a yield of 7.97%.

Both of these corrections will appear on your July statement. We apologize for our delay in processing and thank you for writing to us.

Operations Manager

buried apology

MEMO B: Revised Memo

Good news:
Reference:

Subject: Credit Due
Re: Letter of July 11, 1985

Dear Mrs. Cuskley,

apology:

Thank you for writing us regarding the $37.16 credit we owe you. We apologize for the inconvenience you experienced in the delays and incorrect processing of your accounts.

Documentation:

You will find these two corrections on your July statement:

1. Ready Assets Account
   Credit: $36.33 (yield of 7.97% x 126 days)
   Reason: We credited interest from 2/2/85 to 6/9/85. This is because $1302 was not actually invested until 6/9/85.
2. Margin Account
   Credit: $0.83
   Reason: Adjustment in May charge.

Goodwill:

We appreciate your continued business with ABC Company and again, thank you for writing us.

Operations Manager

3. Model for a Procedure Memo

The most widely used method for writing procedures is called "playscript." Here are the guidelines:

1. Number each step or action chronologically.
2. Begin with verbs for each step.
3. Add an "s" to each verb to soften the message.

The following is an example of an actual procedure memo that was rewritten with the playscript format. Notice that the two main categories of information in a playscript procedure are the person responsible and the action or steps needed.

MEMO A: Original Memo

To: All Bank Employees

Subject: Employee Cardkey

Cardkey #356 should be signed out to bank employees only. It can be signed out only if a bank employee has forgotten his or her cardkey, or reported it lost or stolen.

The procedure is as follows:

1. Employee signs for cardkey.
2. The guard exhanges the cardkey for some form of ID (preferably a driver's license or bank ID).
3. The cardkey is turned in at the end of the employee's day.

Note: The cardkey should not be taken out of the building. The guard can hold the cardkey until the employee returns from lunch (or whatever the case may be).

MEMO B: Revised Memo Using Playscript

To: All Bank Employees

Subject: Procedure for Lost or Stolen Cardkeys

This procedure is to show you the steps you need to take if your cardkey is misplaced, lost, or stolen.

Person responsible:	Steps involved:
Employee	1. Signs for cardkey
Guard	2. Exchanges cardkey for some form of identification: 　　a. Driver's license 　　b. Bank ID
Employee	3. Returns cardkey at the end of the day

The policy is that cardkeys should be signed out to bank employees only. Do not take the cardkey out of the bank.

4. Model for a Proposal

The information that needs to be included in a proposal is the same whether the proposal is one page or twenty pages long. A possible model for a proposal is:

1. Hello
   - Purpose
   - Expectations

2. Background

3. Problem

4. Solution

5. Benefits of the solution

6. Implementation
   - Steps
   - Dates

7. Follow-up
   - Next meeting
   - Phone calls

Following is an example of an informal proposal written by a training director to the director of human resources. Notice that each paragraph has a distinct theme and that all the elements just listed are included on this one page.

Purpose:

Background:

Problem:

Benefits:

Implementation:

Follow-up:

MEMO

Subject: Secretarial/Administrative Skills Training

The purpose of this memo is to update you on progress we've made in implementing the Successful Office Skills training programs for secretaries.

I had a meeting this morning with Barry Martin from the consulting and training firm, Successful Office Skills, Inc. This was a follow-up to the exploratory meeting you and I had with him in March.

I asked Sharon Walsh to attend today's meeting so we could benefit from her knowledge as Employment Manager for the firm. She said that we have a constant problem hiring and retaining qualified secretaries. What's more, we are paying an enormous amount of money to personnel agencies just to find the ones we do have. She is in total agreement with our plan to offer secretarial skills training to our firm's employees.

As I see it, the benefits to the firm are numerous. They include:

- · Increased efficiency and productivity
- · Decreased turnover
- · Improved morale by providing employees with career path
- · Dollar savings in agency fees
- · Preparation for office automated systems

Mr. Martin has suggested that he initially prepare a needs analysis questionnaire. Additionally, he would like to speak to three or four key managers. Sharon will identify those managers who have the greatest need for secretarial personnel. After the data have been accumulated and analyzed, Mr. Martin will suggest what we should offer for training and how best to implement it.

As soon as he receives a go-ahead from us, Mr. Martin will design a questionnaire. He estimates that he will be prepared to begin a needs analysis by the middle of July and that a target date of November to begin training is realistic.

I will call you on Monday, March 31, to discuss how you would like to proceed.

☐ COMMUNICATION PRINCIPLE 8: BE CORRECT

Standard American English is expected in the business world. When we read a memo with a grammatical error, punctuation problem, or misspelled word, a red flag pops up in our mind. Incorrect English is damaging to the reputation and image of a writer because it reflects on his or her credibility, competence, and professionalism. Part of being professional means not making mistakes in your work.

The "Spinach on Your Teeth" Problem

Reading something that is incorrect is similar to watching someone speak who has spinach on his teeth. All we can do is focus on the error (the spinach), not the message. The mistake becomes so distracting that it interferes with communication. The presentation or packaging of a message should be invisible.

We can make three possible assumptions about someone who writes incorrectly.

1. The writer is a careless business person. In working with managers and professionals, I have found that most people write incorrectly out of carelessness. The problem with being careless is that the reader assumes, "If this writer is careless about correctness, she might also be careless in solving my business problems."

2. The writer doesn't know the rules of English. We question writers' general competence when they write incorrectly. We assume that if they haven't learned the rules of English, they may also have trouble learning complex technical or political information. Most people in the 1980s must have at least a high-school diploma to gain entry into the business world. This is supposed proof that they have learned how to read and write. When someone consistently writes incorrectly, we assume that he or she has slipped into the union without paying dues.

3. The writer doesn't consider the reader important. Incorrect writing is also a reflection of a writer's attitude toward the reader.

The unspoken message is "You're not important enough to send a flawless memo to." (You can bet that CEOs don't get careless memos!) At some level, receiving an incorrect memo is a personal insult.

To check for correctness when you write, have reference books readily available. The "bible" for the essential grammar and punctuation rules is Strunk and White's *The Elements of Style* (see the bibliography). It is inexpensive, to the point, and easy to understand. Your second reference tool should be a standard, comprehensive dictionary. Also, check with your local colleges and universities for "grammar hotlines." They are popping up throughout the country and their purpose is to help answer people's niggling grammar and punctuation questions.

Strategies for Being Correct

The following are areas in which competent native English speakers make the most grammatical errors when they write.

1. Parallel Structure

Parallelism is the use of consistent grammatical forms. You use parallel structure as a writing technique when you compare like units of information and want to show their similarity. Writers are forced to use parallel structure when they write procedure memos and "to do" lists. The following examples show the correct and incorrect use of parallel structures. Notice in the first sentence that the flow and rhythm of language is awkward because the sentence lacks parallel structure.

> *Incorrect*:   She likes *to manage* staff and *writing* proposals.
>
> *Correct*:   She likes *to manage* staff and *to write* proposals.

Notice that in both sentences the first verb is "to manage"—the infinitive form of the verb. Therefore the second verb should also be the infinitive form.

Following is an example of parallel structure in a couple of "to do" lists. Notice that in the first list, each word begins with a verb; in the second, each begins with a noun. Both follow the rule of using consistent grammatical forms.

Beginning with verbs:

```
                    To Do:

            1. Call section mgr.
            2. Write DP memo
            3. Study market report
```

Beginning with nouns:

```
                    To Do:

            Collect from staff:
            1. W.W.R. Study
            2. Time cards
            3. 6/1 Status report
```

2. Subject–Verb Agreement

The most common grammatical error made is subject–verb disagreement. If you're unsure about correctness, read your words out loud. Your ear will probably pick up the error. The second approach is more scientific. See if the subject is singular or plural. Match a plural subject with a plural verb form, and a singular subject with a singular verb form.

Incorrect: Special directions and technical data was delivered.

Correct: Special directions and technical data were delivered.

The words "directions and data" comprise a plural subject. Therefore you must use the plural form of the verb.

□ COMMUNICATION PRINCIPLE 9: MAKE YOUR PRESENTATION ATTRACTIVE

We make judgments about a memo before we read one word. These judgments are based on visual appearance. Therefore, memos should be visually appealing. They should have visual balance, order, and organization. A good visual design makes reading look effortless. Attractive memos *invite* the reader to read.

At an unconscious level, we say "yes" or "no" or "maybe" to everything we see. We make gut decisions about what we will put on the top of our "to do" pile and what we will put on the bottom. Either we want to know more about something or we don't, all on the basis of our first impressions. To attest to this gut-level reaction to any memo, during my workshops I have participants say an immediate "yes" or "no" to memos flashed on a screen.

The physical appearance of our writing is the only nonverbal avenue we have for expressing long distance our personality and our standards for professionalism. An attractive memo reflects on its writer. Visual appeal says "I believe in doing things right. My thoughts are organized and uncluttered. I believe in simplicity, not chaos."

In business, the standard for physical appearance for both people and inanimate objects is that they be tidy and clean, giving a sense of order and balance. We become suspicious if the standard is breached. We would question a consultant's professionalism and credibility if he or she walked into the office looking unkempt or too casually dressed. Likewise, if a memo has an unorganized, unbalanced appearance, we are less apt to trust the reader and the message—let alone want to read it.

Your memos are a major aspect of your business image. They are you on paper. And that is why their appearance (as well as their content) is so critical. To ensure their visual appeal, you need to train your secretary to type them with a specific layout. You might keep a file of writing samples that demonstrate the layouts you like best. The key here is to find good secretaries because they will be more inclined to design memos that are works of art.

Strategies to Make Your Memos More Visually Appealing

The following are tips on how to improve the "good looks" of your business memos.

1. Use "Block Left" Formatting

Graphic artists will tell you that the "block left" or "flush left" layout for paragraphs and headings is best because it is the easiest to read. Traditionally, each paragraph is indented five spaces, but this creates a less streamlined appearance. Every company has its own style, but I recommend block left because it has a clean, uncluttered look.

2. Use Short Paragraphs

Long paragraphs are forbidding. Subconsciously our reaction is, "This is going to be hard reading." We tend to write long paragraphs because we learned to do so in school, when they were highly prized. They gave the teacher the message, "I have so much to say."

Notice how you would automatically be drawn to reading the memo on the right, because it has shorter paragraphs.

Long Paragraphs   Short Paragraphs

The following are some guidelines for determining paragraph length.

- Always write a short first paragraph. The reader thus begins with an easy reading task.
- Vary your paragraph length thereafter. However, tend toward short paragraphs rather than long ones.
- Most paragraphs should average approximately the length of one finger joint.

---

3. Use Highlighting Techniques

Studies show that readership increases seventy percent with the use of highlighting techniques. Highlighting techniques are graphic techniques that make important words and ideas stand out. They are road maps that tell readers where they are going and where important stops are on the way.

One technique is to use *white space*. This highlighting method gives the eyes time to rest and time to absorb the information. Facing a page jammed with print is like being bombarded with loud music. Appealing writing does not blast readers with words, words, words, but gives them a few breathers and some peace and quiet on the page.

Another technique is to use *bullets*. You've seen this technique in this book. Bullets are made by striking the letter "o" on the typewriter and then filling in the space. I recommend indenting four spaces to the left of the bullets.

You can also use *headings*. Headings are simply subject titles for the critical paragraphs of a memo. A name I give this highlighting technique is "menu writing." The technique resembles the design of restaurant menus in that critical groups of information are highlighted and then underlined. Journalists and advertisers use the heading technique to grab attention. The benefit of its use is that it gives readers two choices—a fast read or a slow read. If they choose to read quickly, to "scanread," they can get an overview by reading the headings. I have used headings throughout this book.

The following is an example of a memo written with and without highlighting techniques. If you had the choice of which to read, I am sure you would instantly choose the one on the right, which includes highlighting techniques.

MEMO A: Original Memo with No Highlighting Techniques

Subject: Overdeliveries

I refer to your memo dated April 14th addressed to Martha Rovere, covering overdeliveries by ABC Corporation to other brokerage firms. Overdeliveries are caused by numerous reasons. The Margin Department does indeed prepare all delivery bills (2930's), whether original or duplicate instructions. An explanation of the first attached letter to XYZ Company cites that the Cashiers' Department delivered the wrong security. ABC delivered 50 shares of Indiana Electric 14% Cu Pr rather than 50 shares of Indiana Electric 14% Cu *Pfd A* for which the customer is long in his account. The second attached letter is a case of duplicate instructions issued by the Margin Department. We issued these instructions only after we contacted both the receiving broker and Operating Cashiers', and we were advised that no instructions could be located within the Operating Cashiers' Department. The third attached letter is a result of a double punch through our delivery system. Only one instruction was issued by the Margin Department. The fourth letter indicates a duplicate instruction issued by the Margin Department. Our orginial instruction was dated Feb. 13th and our duplicate instruction was dated March 27th. The original instruction could not be located by the Cashiers' Department on March 27th. Delivery was consummated on March 30th and 31st. The last two attached letters were sent to Martha Rovere in error, for we delivered securities and the items were subsequently sold at ABC.

I would like very much to see controls and procedures instituted wherein duplicate delivery instructions are so indicated and brought to a designated Cage person who will fully research the original instruction (copy of which would accompany a duplicate delivery bill) before processing the duplicate instruction.

Many overdeliveries are also noted after extended periods of time have elapsed. Retrieval of such items creates a terrific burden on the Margin Department and more often the items are forwarded to our Legal Department for collection. Therefore, I would appreciate receiving all pertinent research information that generates a CIE with an "as of" date 60 days prior to the date of the entry.

I will be glad to work with you on the establishment of any controls or procedures which will eliminate this problem.

MEMO B: Memo Rewritten with Highlighting Techniques

Subject: Security Overdeliveries to Other Brokerage Firms

This memo has a twofold purpose:

- To explain some of the reasons for overdeliveries by our firm to other brokers.
- To respond to your memo dated April 14, 1985, addressed to Martha Rovere.

What are some of the reasons for overdelivery of securities to another brokerage firm? They are:

1. Duplicate instructions issued by the Margin Department.
2. Incorrect security matched against the delivery bill.
3. Delivery instructions multipunched from the delivery terminal.

Have you ever tried to justify the reasons for such actions? I have.

Duplicate Instructions. Unfortunately this is a necessary evil to provide *service* to our clients. The Margin Department attempts to expedite delivery of the customer's account.

Incorrect Security Match. Comparison between the physical security and the instructions, i.e., security number, cusip number, and description of security, is lacking.

Multipunched Items. Inexperienced personnel work the delivery terminals. New personnel require more supervision.

The Margin Department is indeed responsible for the issuance of duplicate instructions. It issues duplicate instructions ONLY after completion of the following two steps:

1. Check with the receiving broker to verify if delivery was actually made. If delivery was made, the Margin Department researches the item and makes the necessary adjustments to the accounts. If delivery was not made, then:
2. Check with the Operating Cashiers' Department to ascertain that the original instructions are lost within the confines of our firm.

3

The Principles of Persuasive Writing

So far we have studied the basic principles of communication. We have seen that to be effective communicators in both writing and speaking we must be clear, concise, complete, and if possible, brief. These principles remain constant. The next level of communication is persuasion, or the *art* of communication. By applying the guidelines of persuasion to our writing, we are adding the "frosting on the cake" to our communicating skills. The persuasive principles are:

Principle 1. Establish trust with your reader.

Principle 2. Write from your reader's viewpoint.

Principle 3. Get to the point!

Principle 4. Position your ideas.

Principle 5. Use the "Three Messages of Persuasion."

First, let's look at what persuasion is: It's the ability to convince people of our point of view, or at least to get them to *consider* what we have to say, whether spoken or written. You may not think you are in the business of persuasion, but you are. We are all persuaders—

from a crying 1-day old baby to the most sophisticated politician. We are *always* trying to persuade others. Every time we open our mouth or write words on paper, we are trying to influence people, to bring them over to our point of view.

In other words, we are always selling ourselves. In fact, *everyone is a salesperson.* Even if we're not selling a product or service, we are always trying to persuade others to "buy" our ability to think clearly and communicate effectively. Everything we say or write is an attempt to sell our ideas, our point of view, and ultimately, ourselves. In general, however, I prefer the word "persuade" to "sell," because "sell" often has a negative connotation. The difference I see between the two words is that we sell *things* but we persuade *people*. The word "persuade" suggests that our first goal is to relate to people. From now on we will look at all forms of communication as a persuasive process.

Being persuasive gives us control over our lives. We get what we want when we persuade others. When we convince people that our views and solutions make sense, our clients, buyers, managers, and those who report to us want to do business with us. As a result, we feel we have impact and influence on our lives and the lives of others.

☐ PERSUASION PRINCIPLE 1: ESTABLISH TRUST WITH YOUR READER

We need to think of everything we do, say, or write as having one of two effects on others: establishing trust or not establishing trust. You know that if you trust someone, you are open to listening and ultimately to working with that person. People who are in the business of sales and persuasion agree that *the foundation of any sales relationship is trust.*

Trust is knowing that a person's word is good. Trust is when you can say, "I believe you. I believe that you keep your word, that you will do what you say."

In corporate life, establishing trust often becomes more and more difficult as the number of people you deal with increases and the number of people with whom you have personal contact does not. You have less time and opportunity to establish one-on-one trust. Establishing trust through written communication thus becomes critical.

How do you establish trust in writing? By following all the principles of communication that we discussed in the last chapter: being brief, clear, concise, complete, correct, and well organized and by designing visually appealing communications.

However, the best way to establish trust is by speaking with people. Why? Because when we speak to someone, we have the advantage of being able to observe the person's nonverbal cues. We can change our way of presenting ourselves according to our listener's reception so that our listener understands and hears us better. When personal contact isn't possible, the next best way to establish trust is to write.

In my own business, I have found that once trust is established, clients and trainees are ready to share their business concerns. Once there is trust I can persuade and train. Not until there is trust can my clients and I start working together effectively.

☐ PERSUASION PRINCIPLE 2: WRITE FROM YOUR READER'S VIEWPOINT

One method of being persuasive in writing is to write from the *reader's* viewpoint rather than from your own. When you do this, you humanize your writing by showing empathy and understanding for the reader's needs. You tell the reader what he or she wants to know; you address the reader's questions and concerns.

Writing from the reader's viewpoint doesn't mean that you should eliminate writing from your point of view altogether. When you first begin, you need to put on your "writer's hat" and discover your point of view. When you edit, however, you need to put on your "reader's hat." This means conducting your editing sessions with a new slant—taking a hard look at your words from the reader's viewpoint.

Centering on your reader's needs doesn't mean that you should

selflessly ignore your business goals. As the writer/persuader, you must keep your goals in mind and have a definite plan on how to achieve them. The secret is to couch those needs in the words and interests of your reader.

The art of persuasion can most easily be observed by looking at how advertisers work. Advertisements jump out at us in all areas of our lives and in different forms—radio, TV, and print. What makes the advertising industry so successful? The fact that advertisers research their markets. They find out what people need and what makes them tick. They spend billions of dollars each year on marketing surveys, demographic studies, and research to better understand people's needs.

In advertising—which is persuasive communication—the focus is totally on *the other guy*, not on the needs of the advertising agency or the copywriter. The success of advertisers is proof of their ability to understand the needs of their audience and to address those needs.

What if you have multiple readers with multiple needs? In that case you need to write in the graphic style I call "menu writing," using lots of headings to highlight and organize different units of information. You thus provide your readers with reading choices—appetizer, entree, dessert, or drinks. In other words, you're letting readers choose *their* "main course."

Not uncommonly we forget all about the reader and write exclusively from our point of view as writers. Here are three reasons we so easily make this communication error.

1. We Write to Ourselves

Communicating in writing is communicating with the invisible. We face an unseen reader. It's difficult to visualize the person who will eventually read our memo. It's almost like communicating with a ghost. We therefore naturally write to the only person present—ourself.

2. We Become Self-Absorbed

We write from our viewpoint because we are absorbed in our thoughts about writing effectively. Questions pop up like, "Am I saying this right?," or "What word should I use?" We forget the other critical fifty percent of the communication process: the reader. In doing so, we forget about the central questions and needs of the people absorbing the information.

3. The "Bottom Line" Takes Precedence over People

All too often we think only about presenting bottom lines, facts, and figures. We eagerly tell everyone what *our* teams and departments have achieved. The emphasis on bottom-line thinking and writing is one of the current criticisms of many students coming out of MBA programs.

Strategies for Writing from the Reader's Viewpoint

1. Order Information Psychologically

To change your writing perspective and the way you order information, ask the simple question: "If I were the reader, which information would I want first, second, and third?"

People too often are locked into ordering information chronologically rather than persuasively. Why? From habit. And because that is the safest way to order information. Chronological ordering has a firm, verifiable structure. We describe events by starting from the beginning and moving in an orderly way from one event to the next. Almost without thinking, we naturally say or write, "Well, first this happened and then. . . . "

Chronological ordering is appropriate for documenting events. However, psychological ordering, or ordering from the viewpoint of the reader, is more appropriate when you are trying to persuade or answer your reader's question: "What's the point of this memo?" Following are examples of the difference between chronological and psychological ordering.

MEMO A: Chronological Ordering of Ideas

Step 1:
Step 2:

Step 3:

Step 4:

Subject: Sally Jones

On Tuesday, February 21, I was confidentially informed that Sally Jones had recently been hired by ABC Company on a part-time basis.

Well aware of our policy in regard to situations that might lead to conflict of interest, I telephoned the ABC Personnel Department. I first called them on Thursday, February 23, and again on Friday, February 24. In both instances they confirmed that Sally is their employee.

I then phoned Rita Smith of our Employee Relations Department and she did agree that Sally's employment with ABC Company does present a conflict of interest and that she should not be allowed to continue holding a job at both firms.

On Friday, February 24, after consulting you, I decided to terminate Sally's employment with our firm, citing conflict of interest as the reason.

buried main point

MEMO B: Psychological Ordering of Ideas

Readers main concern: *main point up front*

Subject: Termination of Sally Jones

On Friday, February 24, after consulting you, I decided to terminate Sally's employment with our firm, citing conflict of interest as the reason. These are the events that led up to the decision:

Sequence of Events:

—On Tuesday, February 21, I was confidentially informed that Sally Jones had recently been hired by ABC Company on a part-time basis.

—Well aware of our policy in regard to situations that might lead to conflict of interest, I telephoned the ABC Personnel Department. I first called them on Thursday, February 23, and again on Friday, February 24. In both instances they confirmed that Sally is their employee.

—I then phoned Rita Smith of our Employee Relations Department and she did agree that Sally's employment with ABC Company does present a conflict of interest and that she should not be allowed to continue holding a job at both firms.

2. Use Reader's Logic

Order all your sentences and paragraphs in a logical sequence. The logic should be based on the obvious questions the reader will ask as he or she reads your memo.

In the following memo the writer organized ideas from her point of view. In the first sentence she created a question of interest in the reader's mind, but then instead of immediately answering that question, she presented unrelated information. The reader's response to this illogical sequence is, "So what?"

Reader's immediate question: "What are the proposals?"

MEMO A: Original Memo

"So what?"

A representative from Evansville College met with us recently and presented what we feel are some very exciting proposals for a degree program. The college is undergraduate, but it has a working agreement with Becker University for anyone who wishes to pursue a graduate degree. Evansville offers a Business Management Certificate Program that consists of a 30-semester-hour course of study. It also offers numerous courses in many disciplines, including management, accounting, and communications.

MEMO B: More Effective Rewrite

> A representative from Evansville College met with us recently and presented what we feel are some very exciting proposals for a degree program.
>
> Evansville offers a Business Management Certificate Program that consists of a 30-semester-hour course of study. It also offers numerous courses in many disciplines, including management, accounting, and communications.
>
> The college offers undergraduate education, but it has a working agreement with Becker University for anyone who wishes to pursue a graduate degree.

3. *Use the Pronouns "You" and "Your"*

This technique will personalize and humanize your writing. Whenever you write or speak with a "you" orientation, the reader feels important. Some examples of key phrases are:

"You need . . ."

"You suggested . . ."

"You requested . . ."

"Your idea to start a new . . ."

☐ PERSUASION PRINCIPLE 3: GET TO THE POINT!

The way to organize our thoughts when we communicate them in business is to get to the point up front. We shouldn't dawdle.

No one has time to waste in business. That's why we constantly hear people say, "And so, what's your point?," or "Briefly, what are you saying?," or "When you boil it down, what are you getting at?" The truth is that, as decision makers, *we all want the bottom line when given information, just as we want the bottom line when given numbers.*

Good advertising copywriters are masters at getting to the point. They do so because they have precious little space in magazines and on billboards, and precious little time on TV and the radio. This time-and-space constraint forces them to capture the interest of their audience immediately.

When we put our main point at the end of a communication, we usually do so for one of two reasons:

1. We use writing as an act of discovery. Often we place key information toward the end because we aren't sure what we're trying to say. We use writing as a way to explore and discover what we think and how to say what we think. As we write, inspiration hits, and we finally figure out in precise terms what we're really trying to say—two thirds of the way down the page.

2. It's an old way of organizing thoughts. We were taught in school to put the main point—the recommendation, summary, or conclusion—toward the end of our composition. Traditionally we've learned to communicate our main ideas by easing into them. In business, ideas need to be ordered in reverse—main point first and then the details:

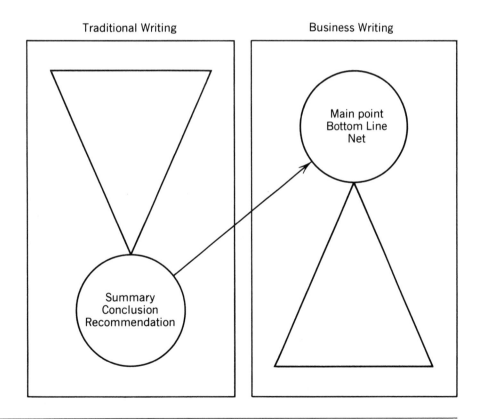

Traditional Writing   Business Writing

Summary
Conclusion
Recommendation

Main point
Bottom Line
Net

Compare the two versions of the following memo. The purpose of the memo is to request the reader to take action in resolving some problems. Note that in the original the request for action is buried at the end; in the rewrite it is positioned up front.

MEMO A: Original Memo

A large number of purchase-order agreements that we received were incomplete. The majority of these had no address listed. In some cases, no name was listed. <u>We need your cooperation in solving this problem</u>.

MEMO B: Revised Memo

<u>We need your cooperation in solving a problem</u>. A large number of purchase-order agreements that we received were incomplete. The majority of these had no address listed. In some cases, no name was listed.

In business writing, this technique of getting to the point is commonly referred to as "frontloading." You can apply frontloading to subject titles, sentences, paragraphs, and whole memos. Frontloading grabs·interest and creates a sense of curiosity in the reader, because the "strong hand" is dealt first. The reader says, "Hey! This gets to the point—I want to read on!" Here is an example of how frontloading can make all the difference in a resume. In the original, the candidate's achievements are buried under the first line of routine information. In the persuasive version, the candidate's achievements are stated first.

Backloaded Achievements

1. Jersey City State College
   Certificate for Academic Excellence,
   1972–73

2. ABC Corporation
   Management Training Certificate of
   Achievement, 1974

3. Jersey City Minority Business Association
   Outstanding Young Businessman of the Year,
   1975

4. XYZ Elementary School of Jersey City
   Member of the Board of Directors,
   1976

Frontloaded Achievements

1. Certificate for Academic Excellence
   Jersey City State College,
   1972–73

2. Certificate of Achievement
   ABC Corporation Management Training,
   1974

3. Outstanding Young Businessman of the Year
   Jersey City Minority Business Association,
   1975

4. Board of Directors
   XYZ Elementary School of Jersey City,
   1976

Strategies for Getting to the Point

1. Frontload Subject Titles

State the main point of the subject at the beginning of the subject title. Usually readers want to know more than just the subject—they want to know *what about* the subject? The "what about" should be placed up front. Here are examples of how subject titles can have more punch.

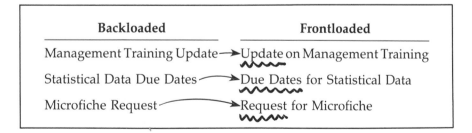

Backloaded	Frontloaded
Management Training Update →	Update on Management Training
Statistical Data Due Dates →	Due Dates for Statistical Data
Microfiche Request →	Request for Microfiche

2. Use Reference (Re:) Headings

After the subject title, try using reference headings. These headings *refer* to previous communications between the reader and writer. Meetings, telephone conversations, and letters can all be referenced. (In some businesses, *"Re:"* means "regarding" and is the same as the subject title—but this is a different use of the heading.) Reference headings appear like this:

> Subject: Purchase of 2 Xerox Copiers
> Re: Your July 14 memo

Use of reference headings to refer to previous communications cues the reader right away to a specific communication. Once focused on your previous communication, the reader is better prepared to move on to the business of the new communication. As a side bene- fit, reference headings are also useful in that they take the place of the standard opener, "As per your July 14 memo . . . ."

3. Frontload Purpose Statements

Get to the main point in the first paragraph! Following is an example of a writer's placing the main point in the last paragraph of the memo. The manager had requested a brief report on a training ses- sion, essentially wanting to know if the writer would recommend this workshop for future use by the staff. Notice how the rewrite is much more powerful, because the reader's question is answered up front.

MEMO A: Original Memo

Subject: Negotiating Training Session

Mike, the Negotiating Training Session was very helpful. From it I learned the following:

1. The four basic elements of a negotiating session, formal or informal, and how to use them.
2. To actively set objectives prior to the session.
3. To recognize the style I use most often and to be comfortable with it.

I did feel more information should have been made available prior to some of the face-to-face training sessions. I also think an additional half day would be helpful to allow more time for prenegotiation preparation.

I would definitely recommend the class for real-estate administrators and project managers.

MEMO B: Rewritten Memo

Subject: Negotiating Training Session

Mike, I would definitely recommend the Negotiating Training Session for real-estate administrators and project managers. From it I learned the following:

1. To identify the four basic elements of a negotiating session, formal or informal, and how to use them.
2. To actively set objectives prior to the session.
3. To recongnize the style I use most often and to be comfortable with it.

I did feel more information should have been made available prior to some of the face-to-face training sessions. I also think an additional half day would be helpful to allow more time for prenegotiation preparation.

Thank you for giving me the opportunity to attend this excellent session.

4. Frontload Paragraphs

Put your lead sentence or topic sentence first in the paragraph. (This is discussed in the section on organizing a paragraph, pages 50–51.)

5. Frontload Sentences

Identify your main point in a sentence and state it right up front. For example:

Backloaded key phrase	Frontloaded key phrase
Due to the limited amount of data available from ABC Company, *the following statistics were not compared with ADS's.*	*The following statistics were not compared with ADS's* due to the limited amount of data available from ABC Company.

6. Backload "Distractors"

Place distracting words at the end of sentences or memos. "Distractors" distract the reader from the main point. Examples are: "Attached is . . . ," "Enclosed is . . . ," "See reference . . . ." When a writer says up front, "Enclosed is . . . ," the reader often feels compelled to flip to the enclosures, and then must start reading from the beginning again.

I suggest mentioning enclosures in less conspicuous positions—either at the *end* of a sentence, in a separate sentence, or toward the bottom two thirds of your communication. That way, as the reader is completing reading, he or she will be ready to flip to the enclosure.

In the following example, notice how the distracting word "attached" begins the first sentence. It detracts from the immediate point, which is to explain the purpose of a manual.

Frontloaded Distractor	Backloaded Distractor
Attached is a copy of the user's manual, which explains in full detail how the system works.	The user's manual explains in full detail how the system works. A copy is attached.

☐ PERSUASION PRINCIPLE 4:
POSITION YOUR IDEAS

The timing of words—where you place them on a page—is everything in persuasion. If you agree that timing of words is important when you are trying to convince people in speech (such as asking for a raise or requesting help on a controversial project), you will also agree that the positioning of words on paper is equally important.

The printed page has several "prime-time" positions. These positions are based on our attention span and on our abilities to remember information and to focus on certain information blocks rather than others. The rule that we naturally follow to remember information I call the "law of the memory." It states:

---

1. You remember best what is first.
2. You remember second best what is last.
3. You may or may not remember what is in between.

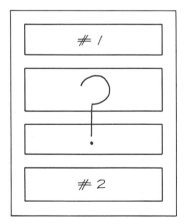

If you think about it, you can probably see that my law applies in your experience. For example, you probably read the first paragraph of a newspaper article carefully, then skim over the middle if the article is of mild interest, and then read the concluding paragraph with more interest.

The first eighty words or so of a memo occupy the most critical position. This means that the memo has to grab the reader up front in the subject title, the first eight lines, or the first paragraph. If it doesn't, the reader will probably stop reading or will read the memo later, with little enthusiasm or none at all.

Three positions have the greatest power on a page: (1) the subject title, (2) the first paragraph, and (3) the left margin (because we read from left to right). The following diagram shows these positions.

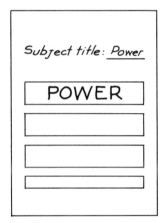

Strategies for Positioning Your Ideas

1. Use Dynamic Subject Titles

Your subject title is your advertising piece. A grabby subject title is one of the most underused power hooks for creating interest. For example:

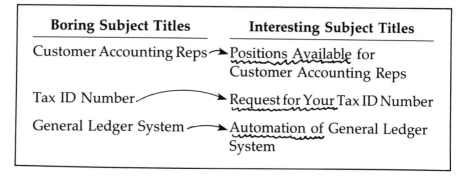

Boring Subject Titles	Interesting Subject Titles
Customer Accounting Reps	Positions Available for Customer Accounting Reps
Tax ID Number	Request for Your Tax ID Number
General Ledger System	Automation of General Ledger System

If the subject title is interesting, regardless of its length the reader will be drawn into the body of the writing. With the Woody Allen film, *Everything You Always Wanted to Know About Sex,* did the eight-word title turn off the audience? You bet it didn't. Woody Allen grabbed us with that long title!

2. Have Interesting Opening Paragraphs

You have a choice among four different messages that will grab attention in your opening paragraph:

a. *A purpose statement*—tell why you're writing (see pages 24–30 for more information).

b. *A benefit statement*—tell what the reader will gain by reading your piece (see pages 87–89 for more information).

c. *A history statement*—tell what occurred before. Here you tell what events triggered this communication. For example, "You requested . . . ," or "As a result of our January 14 meeting. . . ."

d. *A preview statement*—tell what issues or themes the memo will cover. For example, "The two areas covered in this memo are: (1) an explanation of the processing problem and (2) three solutions for solving the problem."

3. Avoid Placing Your Main Point in "No-Man's Land"

The no-man's land that I'm referring to is located next to the last paragraph in your memo:

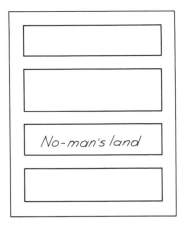

This is dead territory—unless your reader has been a captive audience and has read every word. I'd guess that sixty percent of all business writers unknowingly place their main point in this position. Avoid placing your critical information here unless you are trying to sell an idea in which you know your reader isn't initially interested, or unless you are delivering a tough message.

☐ PERSUASION PRINCIPLE 5: USE THE THREE MESSAGES OF PERSUASION

There are three types of statements of persuasion, and we commonly overlook them when we write. Too often we head directly into the facts and figures and do not consider using these three persuasive devices. They are*:

- Purpose statements
- Benefit statements
- Follow-up statements

*Modified from a sales model developed by Wilson Learning Corp, in a training series on sales, *Counselor Selling*. Used by permission.

These statements help establish trust with the reader. They persuade the reader to consider your point of view because they clarify your goals, motivate the reader, and finally, create action.

You don't *always* use these three types of statements in your writing. Their use depends on individual relationships, the political situation, and the history between you and your reader. Each type of statement is appropriate only in certain situations. You must customize the use of each to your needs as a writer.

These statements come from the three basic questions we all have as readers:

1. Why is this person writing to me?
2. What's in it for me? (What will I learn? gain?)
3. What do I have to do?

You answer the first question, "Why are you writing to me?," with a purpose statement. You tell the reader what's in it for him or her with a benefit statement. And you tell the reader what to do in your follow-up (next step) statements. The following section shows how to use each of the three types of statements in your own writing.

Purpose Statements

Always let readers know up front why you are writing to them. Therefore, use the purpose statement in the beginning. Purpose statements are covered at length on pages 24–30.

Benefit Statements

These statements show readers how their productivity, knowledge base, and effectiveness will improve as a result of reading a memo or using a product, service, or idea. The statements explain what readers will know, learn, or be able to do as a result of their reading. The following are examples of benefit statements.

1. *The benefit to you of buying this portable computer is that it can be stored under a plane seat or can rest nicely on your lap.*

2. *As a result of reading this report, you will know about five new marketing strategies for the next fiscal year.*

3. *Use of this procedure will save you 20 minutes a day in sorting out the chits for travel expenses.*

You must distinguish, however, between benefits and features. Features are the physical specifications of a product. Benefits are the *advantages* of those features, or how the features will enhance someone's life. The key to persuasiveness is to emphasize benefits rather than features.

For instance, I shopped for a business suit recently. The saleswoman told me about the physical features of the suit first, but what really sold me were the *benefits* of those special features. The saleswoman showed me how I could save a considerable amount of money by buying this suit and also eliminate extra time in maintaining it.

Features of the New Suit	Benefits of the Features
Material: Polyester and wool blend	"The material doesn't wrinkle—that means no ironing!"
Color: Dark blue	"The color doesn't show dirt—that means fewer trips to the dry cleaner."
Size: 14 long	"It's a perfect fit—that means no tailor!"

The following is a letter I received from a financial account representative after we met and discussed the possibility of my investing through his firm. The original letter contains no benefit statements, and it is written from the point of view of the writer/seller. Look at the overuse of the pronoun "I." In the rewritten version, notice how the benefits to me, the buyer, are highlighted with use of bullets. The focus has switched from "I" to "you."

LETTER A: Original Letter

Dear Client:

I would like to take this opportunity to welcome you to the ABC Company family. I am sure that our association will prove mutually beneficial. The ABC Company and I both believe that a firm foundation leads to a constructive future. With best personal regards, I am

Sincerely yours,
Account Representative

LETTER B: Rewritten Letter

Dear [Customer's Name]:

Thank you for opening an account with our securities firm.

At our firm, we are dedicated to providing you with these three benefits:

- Sound information for making your investment decisions
- Reliable recommendations that will meet all your financial needs
- Accurate detailed reports of all the holdings in your account

Any additional information we can provide will be made readily available to you. If you have questions, or require any advice, feel free to call me at 237-2828.

Sincerely yours,
Your Account Representative

Follow-up Statements

The third type of persuasion statement tells your reader what the follow-up (the next step) to the memo will be.

The purpose of follow-up statements is to press for action and keep the door open to the next communication. They often appear at the end of the memo and are a natural way to close. Here are examples of follow-up statements.

1. *Please call me regarding this proposal by June 14.*
2. *I will call you March 10 to find out your thoughts on my recommendations.*
3. *Let's discuss this issue in our July 10 meeting.*

Such statements put a new burden of responsibility on the writers who use them. These writers are holding themselves accountable for their actions and responsible for the success or failure of their own work and the work of others.

We often omit these statements when they're necessary because we don't want to appear pushy. Or we omit them because we are not committed to creating action. It makes no sense to spend lots of time writing a memo only to have it sit on someone's desk or float around the office because no one is held responsible for the next step. All the time and effort of writing are wasted if we don't make follow-up statements proposing the next step. Action is less likely to occur. We also lose control over our work flow; flow becomes determined by our reader's agenda, which is probably different from ours. Here's a case study to illustrate the point.

The head of a major training department wrote senior management a ten-page report as to why the training department should be expanded. The report took three weeks to write. The writer did not include a follow-up statement·and so had to wait one month until the manager was ready to get back to him. Simply by omitting that statement, the training manager set himself up for a good deal of unnecessary stress. Without seeming pushy, he could have closed his proposal with "I'll call you this Friday to find out when it will be convenient for you to discuss my suggestions."

The following are three ways that you can press for action or keep an open door to continued communications.

1. Use the Basic Follow-up Statement

With this you simply state to the reader what the next action or step will be. If you can, say *when* that next step will take place; *use specific dates and times.* The formula for the basic follow-up statement is:

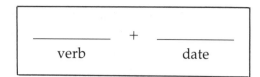

People use dates and times when they feel committed to creating action and to their business goals. The following shows the difference between typical wishy-washy follow-up statements versus explicit, committed follow-up statements:

Wishy-Washy Follow-up Statements

Please advise.

Please get back to me as soon as possible.

Let's get together on this.

This needs to be discussed at your earliest convenience.

Definite Follow-up Statements

I am on your calender May 14 to review our proposal.

I will call you on September 20 to make an appointment.

Please call me on March 13 regarding this delivery.

Using specific dates rather than general time frames lets the reader know what to expect and when to expect it. In the first example that follows, the reader is left hanging; the action could occur anytime from Monday through Friday. The first example also gives the reader an excuse for not being prepared ("Oh! I didn't expect you to call so soon!").

| **Wishy-Washy:** | *I'll call you next week about the research design.* |
| **Definite:** | *I call you on May 6th about the research design.* |

2. Use the Double-Whammy Statement

When action is critical, use double-whammy statements. These statements put the burden of the next step on you, the writer, not on your reader. With these statements, the monkey is on your back two times in a row (once for the written communication, and again for the follow-up). If you leave the action up to the reader, he or she may forget to act or act too late because it wasn't important. If you say, "I'll get back to you," instead of "Please get back to me," you maintain control over the communication.

3. Use the Accessibility Statement

An accessibility statement tells the reader when and how he or she can get in touch with you. It reflects an open-door attitude. An accessibility statement reads like this: "If you have any questions regarding x, y, z, please call me at extension 223." There are two benefits to including this statement. First, the last impression you give is your sincere desire to be available to the reader. Second, you save your reader time by providing your extension number—he or she doesn't have to look it up.

I recommend placing your phone number at the very end of your memo because this leaves a powerful last impression of your sincerity about being available. For example, write "If you want to know more about the cash-flow situation, call me at ext. 492," rather than "Call me on ext. 492 if you want to know more about the cash-flow situation."

Models for Persuasion

The following examples show how a persuasive memo is powerful or weak depending on whether or not the writer includes persuasive messages and develops them. In the original memo, the purpose of each paragraph is confusing. In the rewritten version, each paragraph has one purpose: to state the purpose, to clearly define the benefits, and to press for action (the follow-up statement). (Notice that a problem statement is also included before the benefits are discussed.)

MEMO A: Original Memo

Subject: Acquisition of a Microfilm Processor for the Pre/Post Structuring Department

With the anticipated QXR assumptions in mind, I have been looking at the acquisition of a new microfilm processor to take the place of our present processor which is 10 years old.

The processor that I recommend we purchase is the Deltex Prostar IV. This processor is capable of developing 1 roll (100 feet) of film in approximately 10 minutes. At that rate we would be able to process 6 rolls/hour or 36 rolls/day. The reliability that we experienced in the past 10 years with our present Deltex processor, along with the speed and compatibility with existing hardware, makes me choose the Deltex Prostar IV.

The cost for the Deltex Prostar IV as of 1/3/85 is $10,495 plus tax. The Deltex sales representative has informed me that prices will increase 8-10% by February

I recommend we go ahead and place our order now!

MEMO B: Rewritten Memo

Purpose Statement:

Problem Statement:

Benefit Statement:

Cost:

Follow-up Statement:

Subject: Recommendation for Buying Microfilm Processor for Pre/Post Structuring Department

I recommend that we purchase a new microfilm processor, the Deltex Prostar IV.

We have a major project coming up with QXR and we need a machine that is reliable. Our present machine is 10 years old and Deltex no longer stocks parts for it.

The Pre/Post Structuring Department can benefit from using the Prostar IV in three ways:

1. Speed

   It develops 1 roll (100 feet) of film in approximately 10 minutes.
   At this rate, we could process 36 rolls/day (6 rolls/hour).

2. Reliability

   Deltex gives good service.
   Our present machine has made excellent copies and has been relatively maintenance free.

3. Compatibility

   The Prostar IV is compatible with existing hardware.

The cost for the Prostar IV is $10,495 plus tax (as of 1/3/85). The Deltex sales representative has informed me that prices will increase 8-10% by Februrary.

I recommend we go ahead and buy a Prostar IV as soon as possible, and before the price increases by $1,000. I will call you on January 13 to find out how you would like me to proceed.

double-wammy follow-up

As noted earlier, use of the three types of messages depends on the situation. If your communication goal is to inform rather than to create immediate action, don't include follow-up statements. If you don't want to be called, obviously you should not include accessibility statements.

One final note. Be clear and explicit with your persuasive statements. In this way you give your readers the unmistakable idea that you are writing *to* and *for* them. Often it's a good idea to actually include the words P-U-R-P-O-S-E, B-E-N-E-F-I-T, and F-O-L-L-O-W−U-P. Why? Because it plants the thought in your reader's mind.

4

The Voice of Your Writing

This chapter looks at how you can express your individuality on paper and be both professional and businesslike at the same time. It shows what you have to do to be interesting, personal, and forceful in your writing style. It discusses three areas:

- You and your business writing style
- Selecting effective words
- Choosing the appropriate tone

☐ YOU AND YOUR BUSINESS WRITING STYLE

People get confused about what the word "style" means. The word means the same whether referring to personal style or to writing style. Essentially, style is the sum effect of how a person communicates. Style is a person's manner or personality, whether on paper or in person.

We constantly reveal our style both verbally and nonverbally. We silently communicate our personality through appearance—our hairstyle, our choice of clothes, our way of walking. We also communicate our personality through speech—our tone of voice, speed of speaking, and choice of words.

Our writing also communicates our personality and attitudes—our confidence or lack of confidence, naturalness or stiffness, forcefulness or passiveness. It reveals whether our approach to a problem is personal or impersonal, routine or fresh.

The big problem with many a writer's business writing style is that there is a discrepancy between the real personality and the business writer personality. When people first enter the business world, they naturally copy and learn from their predecessors. They are bound to mimic the style of others. The problem is that often the style becomes petrified. The writers get stuck in the "company style," or even their manager's style. They don't move on, because they don't develop confidence in their writing skills and because they are unsure of where they stand in their work life. Insecurity produces cautious workers and cautious writers.

In Search of the Perfect Style

When writers persist in using a frozen writing style, they feel frustrated, because they're trying to be someone they're not. They copy others' style because they believe that somewhere out there exists "the one perfect style," and that style is *not* theirs.

In fact, your manager, the CEO, and you would each write the same memo differently. The truth is that *the right style is different for each person.* If you wanted to ask your manager for a raise, you might naturally ask a friend to coach you on what to say and how to say it. In the end, though, it will be you who speaks. You enter the communication with your own private career hopes and fears; you use your own words, organize your ideas in a distinctive way; and react uniquely to your manager with every unpredictable second that passes.

The same goes for writing. You have your own writing style that is a direct reflection of you. Thus far that style may have remained undiscovered and dormant! The only way for you to find your style is to *practice* and work at being authentic and honest on paper. Then you will discover that unique, fresh, and spontaneous voice that makes your style distinctive from everyone else's. Once you start going beyond form and business jargon, your memos will begin to ring with your own human, interesting written voice.

The Importance of Creating Uniqueness within Form

There is no question that *we must follow some degree of form in writing*; we must conform to what is considered "acceptable writing behavior" within a company. Using a common language in writing and standard writing formats serves two purposes. It facilitates communication shortcuts and is proof that we belong to the team.

Some examples of necessary standard formats are audit reports, legal documents, procedures for regulated areas in the financial industries, and tax forms. But in most business communication there is room for uniqueness, and that uniqueness is created by individuals.

The truth is that within business *there's a broad range of acceptability in writing and speaking.* Most business people have a gut sense of the range of acceptability for proper business behavior and writing. Breaching this norm is rarely a problem. The real problem is when people adhere too strongly to the company norm. In conforming, they miss out on new possibilities for inspiration, humor, and creative solutions to problems. If we put "proper business writing form" above ourselves and our readers, we are placing facts, figures, form, rules, information, departments, and computers ahead of people.

What Style Do Corporate Leaders Use?

The *Harvard Business Review* ran an excellent article on style by John S. Fielden, entitled "What Do You Mean You Don't Like My Style?" (May–June 1982). According to Fielden, the writing of many high-level executives has three characteristics: It is forceful, interesting, and personal. Leaders must communicate this way so that people will relate to them and be inspired by their leadership.

Strategies for Developing Your Style

Let's look at how you can develop your own style so that you can be more forceful, interesting, and personal.

1. Develop a Range of Styles

Our writing style should change according to our audience. As we change both our clothes and our speech styles for different situations, we must also change our writing style.

Without thinking we adjust our speaking style depending on whom we're talking to. Just think of the range of communication styles you use with the variety of people in your life—business associates, good friends, a spouse, perhaps a religious leader, children, old high school acquaintances, hawkers, new acquaintances, babies—and even pets. Think of how your style would change if you met Lee Iacocca or Ronald Reagan.

Likewise, you need to adjust your writing style according to whether you're writing to upper management, to peers, or to those who report to you. This is where the politics of writing comes in. You are not going to make demands of your manager, nor are you going to grovel with your subordinates. With a superior, you will probably be diplomatic and tactful. With subordinates you will probably be more direct and forceful.

2. Let the Person with the Clout Decide on the Basic Communication Style

The person with the most clout determines what style to use. If the given style is formal and you are informal, your informality will probably seem inappropriate. But being stuffy and formal with people you have contact with every day is also inappropriate. If you find there is a striking gap between writing styles, then you need to find a good, creative middle ground, a compromise between your style and the "preferred" style.

3. Maintain a Constant Style with Each Person

The style of each communication should be set by the tone and feeling of your previous communication. For example, I was consulting with a manager at a financial institution regarding his written communications. We met over lunch and the entire session was open and informal. Two weeks later I received the following impersonal letter from him. This is a good example of how people give themselves up to form.

> *Dear Ms. Sweetnam:*
> *Enclosed herein are the samples of my written correspondence in reference to our April 14th meeting.*
>
> > *Yours truly,*
> > *Joe*

If we had met or spoken over the phone, he probably would have said something personal, like this:

> *Hi, Sherry! Thanks for your helpful ideas in our last meeting. Here are the writing samples you requested.*
>
> > *Joe*

Why not write that? It would be far more appropriate to the situation.

Strategies for Being Forceful

1. Use Short Sentences

You can create a forceful style by encasing your ideas in short sentences and short paragraphs, and by selecting short words. Obviously you want to vary sentence length to avoid monotony. But ultimately, it's best to stay away from long sentences and paragraphs. Short sentences have punch and energy, and they're a welcome relief from the convoluted ones we usually read.

Short sentences also keep you honest. They are great lie-detector tests—they show where you're fudging and where your ideas are foggy.

2. Emphasize Verbs

Verbs bring vitality to your writing. They stress action, movement, life, and decisiveness. In contrast, nouns are void of action. They denote people, places, and things. In business, what really counts is action. Therefore the more active, strong verbs you use, the better. Here are two rules to follow about using verbs.

Rule 1. Recycle nouns into verbs. Verbs are often lurking inside nouns. By recycling your nouns back into verbs, you put new action into your ideas and eliminate wordiness. The greatest "hidden verb" offenders are the "—tion" words. For example:

Actionless	Action
My *promotion* was yesterday.	My boss *promoted* me yesterday.
The purpose of this department is the *distribution* of data.	This department *distributes* data.

Following is a list of nouns that can be recycled back into verbs.

Noun	Verb
consideration	consider
suggestion	suggest
cooperation	cooperate
consolidation	consolidate
rationalization	rationalize

You can identify nouns and verbs by the following common verb and noun markers:

Noun Markers		Verb Markers
-tion	-ance	-er
-ion	-ship	-ate
		-ize

Rule 2. Keep the verb form next to the subject. In the following examples, notice how the force of the verb becomes neutralized and weakened as the subject and verb get placed farther away from each other.

Strongest	*I assist* my co-worker.
	I am *assisting* my co-worker.
	I want to *assist* my co-worker.
	I would like to *assist* my co-worker.
	I would have been *assisting* my co-worker.
Weakest	*I* would like to give my co-worker *assistance.*

The form "I assist" has the most force because the subject and verb are next to each other. The form with "assistance" is the weakest of all six forms, because the action is the farthest of all from the subject, "I."

To summarize, your verbs express less power and action when you use:

1. Helping verbs ("want to," "would like to").
2. Special endings (verb plus "ing," "to" plus verb).
3. Noun forms of the verb ("—tion," "—ance").

3. Minimize Your Use of the Passive Voice

When business writing lacks a forceful voice, it usually is filled with the passive rather than active voice. You read boring phrases such as these: "A meeting is going to be held," "The sales quota was met," "Decisions will be made," "Positions have been adjusted."

Use the active voice as much as possible. But also realize both voices serve distinct and useful purposes. The key is to start consciously choosing between them, rather than routinely using the passive voice.

As native English speakers, we use the active and passive voices naturally and effectively every day. We don't have to understand the grammatical terms "active" and "passive" to use the forms effectively. This classic example shows how even a savvy 3-year-old knows which voice is best:

Passive Voice: Child: *"Mommy, the cookie jar got broke."*
Active Voice: Adult: *"Mother, I broke the cookie jar."*

By using the passive voice, the child abdicates responsibility for breaking the jar and avoids the issue of "whodunit." The adult takes responsibility for breaking the cookie jar by using the active voice.

Often we are not aware of which voice we're using. We use them at a gut level, not at an analytical level. Let's look at the powers of the two voices and how they differ from each other.

The passive voice. In the passive voice, events and situations take precedence over people and their actions. The verb forms are not action oriented but passive, or actionless/passionless. The following are examples of the passive voice. Notice how they are vague as to who or what created the event or situation.

Commitments have been made for the planning session.
Marketing *decisions will be arrived* at on July 14th.
Two *meetings were held* regarding the legal implications.
Fiscal *strategies will be determined* by month end.

The following markers will help you identify the passive voice.

Passive Voice Markers	Example
The word "by"	The news was reported by Dan Rather.
"be" verb plus "-ed"	The questions will be answered today.
"be" verb plus "-en"	Contracts have been written by Legal.

The active voice. In this voice, actions and those who create the actions (or as I call them, the "action creators") are in the limelight. Sentences with the active voice have life—they march, they spotlight the movers and shakers. For example:

The *section manager conducted* the July 14 meeting.

The *midwestern sales rep met* quota.

Express Mail delivers overnight.

The new *clerk adjusted* the position.

1. The active voice indicates who is responsible. It shows right away "whodunit." The passive voice downplays the "whodunit" by omitting it altogether or by placing that information at the end of the sentence. For example:

Active	Passive
Columbus discovered America.	America *was discovered* in 1492.
John broke the sales record.	The sales record *was broken.*
The *board of trustees approved* the budget.	The budget *was approved* by the Board of Trustees.
George transferred to the new unit.	George *was transferred* to the new unit.

2. The active voice shows a direct, forceful request. When writers are addressing those who report to them, or trusted associates (in other words, when they are writing "down" or "across" in an organization), they are apt to use the active voice for requests. But when they are writing to strangers or "up" to their superior and don't want to make a direct request, they use the passive voice. For example:

Active	Passive
Please run 10 copies of the report.	Ten copies of the report *need to be run.*
Please adjust the following security positions	The following security positions *have not been adjusted.*
Please return the merchandise within 10 days.	The merchandise *must be returned* within 10 days.

3. The active voice positions the action and "action creator" at the beginning of the sentence. In the passive voice, the doer is relegated to the end of the sentence and sometimes is completely absent. The doer's importance is subordinated to the power of the event or situation itself.

Active	Passive
Jonathan printed 4 copies.	Four copies were printed *by Jonathan.*
The board reached a new decision.	A new decision was reached *by the board.*

Following is an excellent example of how one writer consciously chose between the active and passive voices to create a nondefensive attitude in the reader. The writer purposefully used the active voice to hold the customer responsible for personal actions. The writer used the passive voice to avoid openly showing blame or pointing the finger.

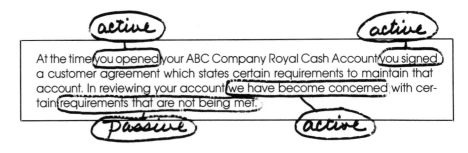

active   active

At the time you opened your ABC Company Royal Cash Account you signed a customer agreement which states certain requirements to maintain that account. In reviewing your account we have become concerned with certain requirements that are not being met.

passive   active

Make the active and passive voices work for you as the preceding example does. You have the choice of deciding what you want to emphasize. Focus the reader's attention exactly where you want it—on the "action creator" or on the event or the result of the action. Being aware of and having control over these "voices" is a major step toward controlling the dynamics of your writing. In general, use the active voice more. You will be amazed at how crisp and alive your writing will become!

To summarize, here is a comparison of the main effects these two voices will have on your writing:

Active Voice	**Passive Voice**
Focuses on "action-creator"	Focuses on event/situation
Pinpoints responsibility	Omits or downplays responsibility
Makes a direct request	Makes a request indirectly
Usually requires few words	Usually requires more words
Sounds informal	Sounds formal

Strategies for Being Personal

1. Use Pronouns

Pronouns humanize your writing. The pronouns are *I, you, he, she, we, they; me, your, him, her, our, their;* and *mine, yours, his, hers, ours, theirs.*

Pronouns bring written communications back to their source—one person talking to another on paper. We use many pronouns in our speech, so why not use more of them in our writing?

When you are strictly presenting information, an impersonal tone is appropriate. For example, in audit reports and compliance reports for the government, there is little room for "I's" and "you's." When you want a personal tone, however, pronouns do the trick.

Don't be afraid to use the word "I." Our parents and teachers taught us to stay away from using "I" for the sake of modesty. However, we've gone overboard in eliminating it from our writing.

2. Avoid Using the Distancing Word "One"

The most impersonal pronoun you can use is "one." It is popular in British English and is considered very formal in American English. For example:

Remote: *One* must sign in at 9:00 a.m. every day.

Personal: *You* must sign in at 9:00 a.m. every day.

Strategies for Being Interesting

1. Be Yourself

The more you are yourself on paper, the more interesting your writing will be. What's important is that you let your self-awareness and sense of humor come across—and then you can't help but be interesting.

2. Write Like You Speak

We are often more interesting when we speak. We tend to speak in colorful, plain English—so why not write in plain English? Don't use formal words just because they sound knowledgeable. The following is a list of formal words often used in writing, paired with their spoken synonyms. Which sound better?

Written Word	Spoken Word
concur	agree
commence	begin
party	person
utilize	use
transpired	happen
subsequent to	after

Look at the difference between the spoken and written form in the following example. The message is "Help!"

Spoken Form:	I'd appreciate your help on this.
Written Form:	This matter requires the attention of Department 406.

The spoken form reflects more of the real you, and is more natural and interesting—so why not use it?

Final Comments about Style

To sum up the points made about style, here is a memo written by Thomas J. Watson, Jr., the past chairman of the executive committee at IBM. This memo has lived on at IBM for over fifteen years because Mr. Watson was able to communicate in a style that was personal, authentic, and creative.

February 19, 1970

Management
Briefing

TO ALL IBM MANAGERS:

A foreign language has been creeping into many of the presentations I hear and the memos I read. It adds nothing to a message but noise, and I want your help in stamping it out. It's called gobbledygook.

There's no shortage of examples. Nothing seems to get finished anymore—it gets "finalized." Things don't happen at the same time but "coincident with this action." Believe it or not, people will talk about taking a "commitment position" and then because of the "volatility of schedule changes" they will "decommit" so that our "posture vis-a-vis some data base that needs a sizing will be able to enhance competitive positions."

That's gobbledygook.

It may be acceptable among bureaucrats but not in this company. IBM wasn't built with fuzzy ideas and pretentious language. IBM was built with clear thinking and plain talk. Let's keep it that way.

Tom Watson Jr

Reprinted by permission of Thomas J. Watson, Jr. © 1970.

☐ HOW TO SELECT EFFECTIVE WORDS

When we're struggling for words, we often believe that somewhere there exists "the perfect word." Actually, there's no such thing as the perfect word. Rather than worrying about striving for perfection, the practical question for us to ask is, "Which word communicates the best?"

All of us have our favorite words based on our personal taste. And taste in words is about as predictable as taste in ice cream. We also select our words on the basis of experience. Our choice is influenced by the words we heard and used at the dinner table while growing up, the words our community uses, the words that are popular in our region of the country, and the words that are well respected in our business environment.

Words are an integral part of our identity, so telling people what kinds of words to use is very tricky business. In one case study at a major Wall Street firm, a manager encouraged his subordinates to use a certain list of words and to avoid others. For example, he said, "From now on, use the word *agree*, not *concur*." People rebelled. Why? Because being told what words to use was like being told what color socks or skirt to wear.

If a word doesn't communicate a writer's intention, the writer has good reason to change it. However, if a word *does* communicate and its use is argued simply as a matter of style difference (for example, the difference between *concur* and *agree*), then the writer must decide how deeply committed he or she is to that particular word.

Your Words Control How People React to You

Once you begin to analyze the written word, you begin to realize the tremendous impact that words—both written and spoken—have on people. Our words create thought in people's minds. If you want to trigger a particular thought, you use the word that will plant that thought. For example, if you want people to respond to you in a positive way, polite words such as *please* and *thank you* work wonders. Likewise, if a child is angry about something, your asking her, "Are you angry?" only makes her focus on the existence of her anger and further verifies and justifies it. If you don't ask the question in the first place, very likely her mood will pass because it has not been acknowledged by either spoken or written word.

Beware! Words Are Battlegrounds

When business people fail to develop a cooperative relationship, they often find it difficult to discuss their differences. One arena where people do express their differences is that of word selection. Arguing over words seems less of a blatant, frontal attack than criticizing someone personally. Words become symbolic of differences and cause alienation in business relationships.

For instance:

An English friend working for a New York law firm repeatedly used the word "whilst" in his reports to American clients. The senior partners would circle the word and put a question mark beside it. My friend took this as a challenge that "his" word was wrong. What the editor/reader was trying to say was, "This word jumps out at me and shows that we are from different countries. It emphasizes our differences rather than our similarities. Please use words that our clients feel comfortable with." Unfortunately, the use of this word developed into a battleground for proving which language was "right," British English or American English.

So remember: *Word battles are often contests for proving whose language or background is right or wrong, and ultimately, which person is right or wrong.*

Strategies for Selecting Effective Words

1. Avoid Routine Business Jargon
There are two types of business jargon:

1. Specialized vocabulary used by those in the same line of work.
2. Long, roundabout words or phrases.

Professional and technical business jargon is a language shortcut and is effective as long as the reader and writer speak the same language. It is composed of the buzz words used by people in a certain profession or work place. It's a type of "club" language for members. For example, computer people refer to "booting up," "loading," "bytes," and "bits." IBMers talk about "communicating net" (which means getting to the point). They also speak of "copy machines," not "Xerox machines" (if you make this mistake, you're told to "byte thy tongue"). Merrill Lynchers speak of "OLP," their home office address, One Liberty Plaza.

The second type of jargon is roundabout, overused business language. For example:

pursuant to	*for your information*
as per	*effective immediately*
enclosed please find	*please be advised*
in accordance with	*in terms of*
we have been informed that	*in response to*

What's the problem with using routine business jargon? It's boring. The phrases have lost their impact because they've been written or spoken thousands of times before. Further, this jargon heightens the problem of people feeling dehumanized because it's boilerplated and not authentic. People want words that reflect a real person, not a cold, vacant writer.

The idea of eliminating routine business jargon from business writing causes concern for some people. They have a hard time letting go of jargon for the following reasons:

1. It's safe. Everyone else seems to use it, so it must be okay. People are afraid that if they use natural, nonroutine language, they won't be considered professional. They are afraid they will sound unbusinesslike without these words.

2. It's familiar. With use of business jargon, people don't have to think about what to say. They just begin with a tried-and-true cliche: "As per our conversation of April 14."

3. It's a way to get started. Most business jargon is found in the first paragraph, at the beginning of other paragraphs, and at the end of the closing paragraph. Use of jargon is an easy way to get started and to sign off. (If this is your habit, you don't necessarily have to give it up—but do edit it out later on.)

What should you do if your manager believes in business jargon and thinks you should use it too? First, you must know your own philosophy about the use of jargon. If you decide that it isn't effective for you, you need to train your manager tactfully and show him or her subtly that nonjargon language is more effective. Last, if you and your manager disagree on the use of certain words, you must decide which word battles to fight. Some aren't worth it, others are.

To avoid jargon, try using pronouns. Pronouns force the use of a more authentic voice. Notice this in the following examples.

Jargon	Natural
Pursuant to our agreement . . .	*We* agreed . . .
As per our conversation . . .	As *we* discussed . . .
In accordance with your request	*You* requested . . .

2. Change General Words to Specific Ones

When words are very general, they are vague. Use of specific words can be especially helpful in your closing paragraphs. Here are examples of routine closings (note the emphasized general words).

Thank you for your *assistance* in this *matter*.

Thank you for your *cooperation*.

Call me if you have any *questions*.

Should you have any further *questions* regarding this *situation*, please give me a call.

The secret is to turn these general closings into specific ones. For example, the words *"in this matter"* are very general. They refer vaguely to "all that I've written above." Why not repeat in concise terms *what* the "matter" is? The advantage to this is that your last words to the reader reinforce the exact action you want to instigate. Here are examples of general language (emphasized) turned into specific language.

Routine Closing	Nonroutine Closing
Thank you for your cooperation *in this matter*.	Thank you for your cooperation *in completing the Statement of* Requirement Forms.
Please contact me if you *have any questions*.	Please contact me at ext. 35 if you have any questions regarding the dates of the workshops.
Please proceed with *this recommendation*.	Please proceed with our recommendation of installing the dock lifts.

Sometimes a specific goodbye sounds repetitive in a short memo. When this happens one option for avoiding jargon in closing sentences is to simply write "Thank you."

To prove the point that you don't have to write with jargon, following is a routine business letter and two viable rewrites using more personalized, natural language.

MEMO A: Original Memo with Jargon

Re: Margin Account #852–3479

Dear Mr. and Mrs. Donaldson:

In reference to your above account with ABC Company, *please be advised* that on November 18, 1984, a deposit was credited to your account in error. A check was then sent to you on January, 12, 1985, which was also in error.

Please remit a check to ABC Company for $500.00 to cover the debit in your account. *Enclosed find copies* of the above statements and an envelope *for your convenience*. If you have any problems with this request, please call (212) 555-0543.

Sincerely yours,

George Carter
Manager

MEMO B: Revised Memo—Version 1

Re: Credit error Account #852–3479

Dear Mr. and Mrs. Donaldson:

We incorrectly credited your Margin Account with the ABC Company for $500 on November 18, 1984. We further complicated matters by sending you a check for that amount on January 12, 1985.

Would you please send us a check to cover the debit in your account?

Please call me if you have any questions. (212) 555-0543

Sincerely yours,

George Carter
Manager

MEMO C: Revised Memo—Version 2

Re: Account #852–3479

Dear Mr. and Mrs. Donaldson:

I'd like to apologize for a processing error that occurred in your account. This resulted in your erroneously receiving a check for $500.00. The errors occurred as follows and appear on the enclosed statements:

1. 11/18/84—A deposit for $500.00 was credited to your account in error.
2. 1/12/85—A $500.00 check was mailed to you in error.

As a result, a check for $500.00 is needed to clear the debit in your account.

Your prompt remittance of these funds will be appreciated. If you have any questions, please call me at (212) 555-0543.

Sincerely yours,

George Carter
Manager

3. Use Words that Create Mental Images

Select words that create in your readers' mind the same visual image that you have in your own mind. Your goal is to get your readers to "tune into" your picture. For example, if your goal is to nudge your readers to act, you must choose words that create a picture in their mind of their actually doing what you want them to do. For example, suppose you want someone to send you a check. You write the routine phrase for requesting transmittal of a check: "Please remit a check for $29.95." The problem is that *"remit"* does not create a clear visual image in the reader's mind. (What is the action of "remit"?) You need to choose a word that will create the image of the reader going to the mailbox and sending a check. Here are a range of possibilities.

Which word creates the exact image in your reader's mind that you want? Probably "write" or "mail." The word "write" conjures up an image of someone actually sitting with a pen and a check and writing. *"Mail"* conjures up the image of putting a stamp on an envelope and of dropping the envelope into the mailbox. These words work much better than the word "remit." Isn't it amazing how easy and obvious choosing the right word can be? This is just common sense and plain English.

4. Try to Avoid Negative Words

I call negative words "red flag" words. These words cause the reader's blood pressure to go up. What is negative depends largely on the situation and on the reader's and writer's relationship. For many, words like "tax" or "IRS" are very negative. Obviously, unpleasant and negative situations and words cannot always be avoided—in fact, they must be addressed before business problems can be solved.

The lesson here is to realize what reactions you create in readers when you write negative words. When you use them, you run the risk of not being heard. Readers will often focus on the one negative word and miss the larger picture. For example, when a customer service rep writes a long and conciliatory letter to a complaining customer and slips in, "I'm sorry for the minor difficulties you experienced," the word "minor" negates all the good intentions of the writer and damages the business relationship. In customer service, there is no such thing as a minor or unimportant problem.

One of the greatest challenges for any communicator is the problem of expressing a negative message in positive words so that the message is both heard and received in a positive manner. Think of the possibility of going through life being effective, powerful, and diplomatic, yet being able to avoid the word "no."

Here is an example of how one soft-drink company significantly increased its sales by simply removing the word "no" from its ad copy.

Old Copy	New Copy
This cola has no sugar.	This cola is sugar free.

The word "no" makes buyers automatically assume that something has been taken away, while the word "free" is associated with a gift. Here are other examples of negative messages being rewritten to use the "power of positive writing."

Negative	Positive
Don't smoke!	Please smoke outside.
You failed to sign the agreement	The agreement was returned unsigned . . . .
To avoid the loss of your good credit rating	To preserve your good credit rating . . . .
We don't give refunds if the returned item is dirty.	We gladly give refunds if the item is clean.

For the sake of awareness, here is a list of potentially loaded negative words (notice how *you* react when you read them).

mistake	should	not
fail	waste	never
oversight	you must	unfortunately
no	neither	problem

5. Avoid Slang and Overly Casual Language

Use words that are appropriate to the business environment (but not, of course, routine business jargon!). Our English language of over one million words has many different categories of words: sports words, religious words, political words, teenage slang words, romantic words. Choose words that are acceptable and appropriate for business. The following is a real example of a totally inappropriate word choice for a business environment: *"No way are we going to be suckered into buying a second-class machine."*

6. Use Words Your Reader Is Familiar With

New words make readers uneasy. When we read words we don't know, we have fleeting thoughts about having missed a Harvard education. New words point out to us what we perceive as educational and social gaps between the writer and ourselves.

Unfamiliar words also distract readers. Readers concentrate entirely on the new words while the point of the sentence slips away. Some disciplined readers stop reading and go to the dictionary. But many don't have the time. The result is that the unfamiliar words have hindered communication between the writer and the reader.

Often writers use big words because they feel this elevates their status and educational background. What happens when we read impressive words? We are turned off, because we feel the writer is trying to show off.

Along this line, *don't use technical language with a nontechnical reader*. Too often people write using the language and specialized vocabulary of their field. When writers use words that only insiders know, they cut off communication. How many times have you read insurance policies, legal papers, tax forms, financial plans, and computer manuals that were Greek to you? The words were clearly English but they didn't make sense. I call this English-as-a-secret-and-foreign language.

Summary about Words

When you are trying to select the best word, ask yourself these key questions:

- Which word communicates best to my reader what I'm trying to say?
- Does using this word unify me with or separate me from my reader?
- Is my idea the centerpiece it should be, or does any word I've used stand in the way of communicating my idea?
- Will any word I've used distract my reader?

Follow these three essential word rules:

1. When in Rome, speak and write as the Romans do.
2. Let the viewpoint of the reader determine what words you use.
3. Choose words that blend, rather than distract.

And follow the Golden Rule of Communication:

COMMUNICATE TO EXPRESS, NOT IMPRESS!

☐ HOW TO SELECT THE APPROPRIATE TONE

What is tone? Tone is the emotions, attitude, mood, or feeling that our words convey. The tone of our writing is the same as the tone of our voice. In both cases, tone reveals if we're excited, interested, angry, disappointed, bored, frustrated, apologetic, optimistic, open, disgusted, hopeful, or determined.

When we write, we are handicapped in fully expressing ourselves and our emotions, because we lack such nonverbal communication cues as voice and facial expressions. The only cue we have is the words we choose to put on paper. This explains why each written word has so much more clout than does each spoken word.

It is hard for writers to hide their feelings, even if they try to bury them under mountains of words. When you are sure of yourself and your work, your writing reflects confidence. Your words have a positive and forceful ring. If you feel unsure of where you stand with your reader and your subject, your tone will be more formal, routine, and stiff, and you will tend toward wordiness. Just one word can tip off the reader to your inner attitude.

1. Tone Should Be Appropriate to Business Relationships

Tone is determined by your relationship with your readers and by your position in an organization. If you are writing to a superior, you will probably be diplomatic and tactful in tone. If you are writing to a subordinate, you will probably be more assertive and direct.

Let's see how tone is determined by the relationship between the reader and writer. In the following example, the basic message is "Help!" Notice how the first example is brief and friendly, the tone informal because it is written to a trusted co-worker. In the second example, the request is wordier and has a more formal tone, because it is written to a higher ranking manager who is a stranger.

Friendly tone:	Liz, I'd appreciate your help in this matter.
Formal tone:	This matter requires the attention of the department.

In the end, you have to choose the tone that will achieve your business goal.

2. Tone Should Be Natural

Given a choice between a formal and a natural tone, I recommend the natural tone because it reflects the way you would speak to someone. A formal tone may be appropriate if your reader or superior expects it. But in most cases business writers tend to be overly formal. This makes it hard to find the real person underneath the words, and readers are easily bored.

3. Tone Should Be Positive

Use what I call "power words," words that create positive responses in people and make them more apt to listen to you and accept your ideas. Some examples are:

> Here are three *benefits* to you. . . .
>
> The *solution* to this long-standing problem is. . . .
>
> *Thank you* for your *help.*
>
> We are *committed* to giving you good *service.*

☐ HOW TO WRITE "TOUGH MESSAGES"

Sometimes negative messages are unavoidable. The question is, how do you say *no* diplomatically? Timing is crucial when you have to say no. One answer is to use the KKK method. KKK stands for

> **KISS**
> **KICK**
> **KISS**

In other words, follow this formula:

> 1. First say something kind to your reader.
> 2. Then give your tough message.
> 3. Then close with a kind remark to soften the blow.

In essence, you sandwich your negative message between the positive messages. You can use this approach in all your communications, verbal and written. (It is an excellent approach in writing performance appraisals.)

The following two letters are examples of how drastically the impact of a letter changes depending on the positioning of the "kick."

Letter That Starts with a Kick

Kick:

Kick:
Kiss:

> Dear Kathy: *Red Flag*
>
> We are (not) going to use your services on either the Group Representative Insurance Development System project or the Contract Analyst Training System project. We feel that neither project is the best use of your time and skills for us.
>
> If in the future we have a project suited to your talents, we will contact you.
>
> We appreciated your very detailed and well-written proposals. We were glad to have the opportunity to talk with you, as well as to see your work.
>
> Sincerely,

Rewritten Letter That Starts with a Kiss

Kiss:

Kick:

Kiss:

> Dear Kathy:
>
> We appreciated your very detailed and well-written proposals. We were glad to have the opportunity to talk with you, as well as to see your work.
>
> I am sorry to say we will not be able to use your services on either the Group Representative Insurance Development System project or the Contract Analyst Training System project. We feel that neither project is the best use of your time and skills for us.
>
> If in the future we have a project suited to your talents, we will contact you.
>
> Sincerely,

In the original letter, the writer places the kick up front to "get to the point." The word "not" in the first sentence sets up a negative tone for all that follows; many readers would throw this letter away and be left with a negative impression of the writer and the company. In the rewrite, notice how the writer's beginning with a kiss leaves the reader with a positive attitude.

Wise mothers use the KKK method on their children. For example, suppose your 4-year old daughter Jill has some beautiful tulips in her little hands. They did not come from your garden. They obviously came from the Bennetts' garden across the street. Using the KKK method, you say, "Jill, you know how much I love you [kiss], but stealing flowers from the neighbor's garden is wrong, and I'm very disappointed in what you did [kick]. Now, go and apologize to the Bennetts and let's forget about this. Let me give you a hug [kiss]."

Don't overdo it, though. When you have a negative to deliver, don't lead your reader on with kiss after kiss. In the following tough-message letter, the reader reacted negatively because it took the writer too long to get to the point (note the reader's "inner editor" comments written in the margin):

So what!

Dear Andrea:

Why pussy foot around? Get to the Point!

Preliminary interviews for our Sales Training Program have stretched relentlessly beyond our first, then a second, cut-off date. It is hard to comprehend that so much activity could have been squeezed into the weeks since our first conversation. It is time now to report back to you on the next phase in the selection process.

The final round of interviews will begin November 9th and end November 28th. We will invite 25 candidates to return for formal meetings with sales managers from three divisions. These finalists offer an exceptional blend of sales, media, and promotion experience.

Took him 2 paragraphs to get to the Point!

We regret being unable to include you in the next round of interviews. This was a most difficult decision. Remember, please, the Sales Training Program will continue on an annual basis. Interviews for the Class of 1987 will begin in the fall. We would like very much to reevaluate your file at this time.

Thank you very much for your time and interest. You have our best wishes.

Sincerely yours,

Bill Bower
Associate Director
Sales Training Program

yeah!

Really?!

The lesson is that when people kiss, kiss, kiss us and *then* kick us, we feel angry. We feel caught off guard, tricked and manipulated. The secret is to give a *quick* kiss, and then get on with the kick. Be thoughtful of your reader, but also be straightforward!

5

The Process of Writing

So far we have looked at the science and the art of written communication. The next step is to look at the process of writing. This chapter deals with the *real* reason most people feel they have to work on their writing—the fact that they find writing a chore. They want writing to be easier, faster, and more fun. I've designed some strategies to help people do just that—write faster, with more ease, and even have fun while they're doing it.

Many people say they don't like to write. I don't believe it. I believe that people like to write once they get started. The trick is to start. They need to turn the writing switch *on*, and the rest will take care of itself. What happens when people start writing? They find it hard to stop, because:

1. The spirit and rhythm of writing take over. We become so involved in expressing ourselves and communicating our ideas that we forget we are even writing. All that exists is thought and observation: seeing how one idea surprisingly connects to another, discovering new ideas, observing how old and new ideas mushroom and merge to make up larger pictures and patterns of thought.

2. Writing is a rich channel for self-expression. A universal human frustration is the inability to articulate our feelings and thoughts. Writing helps us to clarify our thoughts. Writing forces us to come clean with what's on our mind. When we do express ourselves effectively on paper, we feel a sense of relief.

3. Writing is a refuge. Normally our workdays are spent reacting to the external world and putting out fires. We seem to have unending demands at work: from our managers and those who report to us, from telephone callers and stacks of reading materials, and from the umpteenth problem to solve.

Writing allows us to shut out the world. It gives us a valid excuse to shut our office door. We have the luxury of looking inward instead of outward. The creative process begins to work. During these good moments, writing becomes a resting place, a healing time.

4. Writing is an unpredictable adventure. We discover thoughts we didn't know we had. Our writing is unpredictable because our thoughts are unpredictable. For example, can we predict exactly what we will say in any given situation, or exactly what we will be doing at 3:00 this afternoon, or what we will be saying during our next phone call? Of course not! Life is unpredictable, and so is writing.

☐ GETTING STARTED

Writing isn't the toughest part of writing—getting started is. There are three phases to getting started: (1) ending procrastination, (2) psyching yourself up to write, and (3) actually getting started.

Ending Procrastination

We all avoid writing at times. Often we spend more time procrastinating than we do actually writing. When we finally do start, it's the eleventh hour.

Let's look at a typical scenario. Pretend that it's 9:00 a.m. Tuesday morning and you just realized you have to get a key memo out to your manager by Friday. The following is a typical approach to getting the memo written.

Scene 1.   You worry. Thoughts run through your mind: "I wish I didn't have to write! I'd rather be at the conference than having to grind out this memo! What will I say—and how am I going to say it? What can't I say? Why do I have to write? Maybe I'll just make a quick phone call . . . " And so on.

Scene 2.   As your worries escalate, you do the most natural thing: get a cup of coffee or tea. Afterward you make more phone calls, read memos from the "in" basket, or call meetings. All the while you rationalize that these low-priority tasks are necessary and might as well get done. You also tell yourself that even though you aren't writing now, you will do it later in the day. You convince yourself that you produce better under pressure anyway.

Scene 3.   The workday ends, and you haven't put one word on paper. You firmly resolve to start writing tomorrow, when you will be "really prepared—mentally and physically." The next day you repeat the same pattern and the heavy, sickening feeling of guilt and the dread of writing intensify.

We pay dearly for procrastinating. First, *the longer we procrastinate, the harder it is to start writing*. Procrastination brings on feelings and thoughts of "I hate to write!" These feelings intensify our resistance to writing. Procrastination also causes unnecessary stress and guilt, because we're not doing something we should be doing. Finally, we never are able to reach our writing potential, because we never give writing our best effort and prime time.

You can use the following strategies to get over procrastinating.

1. Admit to yourself that you're procrastinating. Recognize the symptoms of procrastination when they occur. Say out loud to yourself, "Well, here I am procrastinating!" Acknowledging the reality brings you closer to stopping procrastination.

2. Stop worrying—start writing. The Army has a system to help some recruits overcome fear: When paratroopers are afraid to jump from an airplane, the Army tells them to jump, jump, and jump again until they're no longer afraid. If you find you're anxious about writing, the only way to get over it is to write. A slogan to help you overcome your resistance to writing is: The only way to fight is to write!

Once you stop procrastinating and actually sit down to write, your next hurdle is the blank page. You sit at your desk with pencil and paper in a quiet room and you look at this:

A common reaction is to run. This is called . . .

Blank Page Panic

Psyching Yourself Up to Write

Just as you psych yourself up to exercise or diet, something you'd rather not do, you need to psych yourself for writing. You can prepare your mind and surroundings in several ways:

1. Clean Up Business Details so You Can Concentrate
Take care of crucial details that keep you from concentrating. By cleaning up your "to do" slate, you can approach writing with a peaceful mind.

2. Set Up Chunks of "Procrastination Time"
Allow yourself the luxury of *some* procrastination. Easing into writing is perfectly legitimate. Just resolve that you will start writing at a particular time. And stick to that resolve. Then you can enjoy your moments of procrastination.

3. Surround Yourself with Your Favorite Things
You're psychologically more ready to start writing if you have comfortable, pleasant surroundings with your favorite "things" around

you. Create a sense of "holing up" by setting up a homey atmosphere. Have not just your favorite pencil and paper but your favorite mug, your favorite pictures, your favorite whatever-it-is nearby.

4. Do Something Nice for Yourself Before You Write

Whatever it takes to get psychic energy, do it. For me, it's preparing a hot mug of tea or taking a walk. For others, it may be chugging down a soft drink or calling a friend.

5. Make Writing Convenient

Make writing so convenient that you don't have to waste one extra second trying to find pencil or paper. Writing should be only a hand movement or a chair swivel away. Have pencil and pad at your fingertips routinely, 24 hours a day. Have your writing tools not only on your desk or within reach but in your briefcase, pocket, or purse—even next to your bed.

6. Buy Classy Pens, Pencils, and Stationery

Using classy writing gear will help you feel good about writing. It will reinforce that you value and honor the act of writing. Choose one "special" pen you can use for special occasions: attending meetings, signing important written communications. When you use your classy business pen, it's like wearing your best business suit.

7. Have the Proper Writing Tools

Have these writing tools within easy reach:

- Pads of legal paper
- Post-it notepads
- A healthy supply of the kinds of pens and pencils you like to write with
- The writing equipment you feel most comfortable: with: typewriter, dictating machine, or a word processor

8. Learn How to Use a Word Processor

The word processor will revoluntionize your ability to write productively and effectively. These two pieces of advice will help you get accustomed to it:

- **Keep the System Within Easy Reach**
  The more accessible the computer is, the more you will use it.
- **Keep the System on throughout the Day:**
  If you keep your computer on all day, you are psychologically more apt to use it. You don't have to waste time booting up the operating system and calling up the files you need.

9. *Plan a Reward for Yourself After You've Gotten Started*

Plan to treat yourself for having gotten started. You will then look more forward to getting started rather than dreading it.

Actually Getting Started

Getting started writing is just like getting started swimming. The thought of the initial plunge makes us shudder. But once we're in, we're so involved in swimming, the feel of the water, the fluidity of our body, and our pleasant thoughts that we forget about how much we hated the shock of that initial cold plunge.

Getting started is easy when the risk isn't high. We write "to do" lists or postcards without a second thought. But to write a report to the CEO or a tough-message performance appraisal takes the gritting of teeth to get going.

You have one critical objective and one objective only when you first sit down to write: TO GET WORDS ON PAPER. Even if the words turn out to be one word scribbled on a cocktail napkin, you have gotten started. With that one word, you have begun to create.

The problem is that people put constraints on getting started. Some think that having a perfect start will make all the difference between writing well and writing poorly. Others believe they must write their first paragraph first. Not so. The Golden Rule for Getting Started Writing is: "There is no rule about where to start. Just start where you feel comfortable."

Start writing the known and comfortable and then proceed to the unknown and uncomfortable. Start with whatever subject or idea you like, whether it's at the beginning, middle, or end of your memo. This may mean that you'll begin in the middle, write toward the end, and then go back to the opening paragraph.

It doesn't matter how you proceed. The truth is, *No matter where you start, you'll end up in the same place.* Exploring the ideas inside your head is like following tributaries—eventually you come to a river.

All your ideas are already present. They are bubbling, brewing, and boiling away under the surface. Your brain contains an imprint of all your past personal and work experiences and your point of view about the world. Your ideas are an interrelated mishmash of associations. All these ideas trigger and activate each other. All you must do to discover them is get started. No one really cares about *how* you get started—it's the final product that counts.

☐ PUTTING THOSE WORDS ON PAPER

There are two equally effective approaches to writing, and writers often switch from one to the other. The one chosen depends on the approach the writer is most comfortable with, the amount of time the writer has available, and his or her knowledge of the subject, comfort level with the reader, and intuitive strategies for creating.

Approach 1.   Create a Plan

Some people start with a plan (the word "plan" is less intimidating than the word "outline"). They want organization and form to their thoughts before they begin writing in sentences. Often they are clear about their ideas because they have given them a great deal of thought.

Approach 2.   Write, Write, Write

Some people just write, write, and write, spilling their thoughts onto the page like a stormy downpour. I call this the "cathartic method" or "the spill-your-guts method" or "the blaaaaaaaaaaaah approach" to writing. In this approach people discover their point of the view and creative ways to express it. Later they go back and categorize and organize the information into a clear plan (or outline). With this approach the opening paragraph is often the last to be written.

Three Strategies for Getting Words on Paper

1. Write Purpose Statements

Start with the old standby: "The purpose of this memo is. . . ."

2. The Sweetnam R4 Method (Run Right to the RestRoom)

The essence of this strangely named method is, "Write things down while they're *fresh* in your mind." Where did the name originate? From a true story about the negotiation style of diplomats at the United Nations. It is against protocol for diplomats to take notes during negotiation sessions. Looking down at pad and pencil prohibits constant eye contact, which detracts from the establishment of trust.

As a result, bathroom breaks are frequent. Negotiators are always running to the restroom and can be seen madly jotting down notes from their discussions. These diplomats understand the importance of writing things down while they're fresh and accurate in the mind. You, too, need to write things down while they're fresh—during meetings and interviews and research sessions.

Some of your richest writing moments are the seconds after you've had a brilliant idea or insight. It's then that your ideas are their most potent. Since ideas spontaneously come and go, you need to capture them at their crest, before their power and momentum are dissipated and lost.

You'll find getting started much easier once you start consciously using the Sweetnam R4 Method. You'll find yourself writing notes before you go to sleep at night, while you're eating lunch, in elevators, and during meetings. Each time you do this, you will in fact have gotten started on your next writing task.

3. The Jean Bubley Dialogue Method

Write down all the questions you think your reader would have. For example, your reader would ask, "Why are you writing to me?" "What do I have to do?" "What's your point?" After you write the questions, the answers naturally flow.

That is how I wrote much of this book. I chose a personal friend and business associate (Jean Bubley) whom I consider representative of the kind of person who would read this book. Whenever I got stuck, I reverted to this question-and-answer technique. Here is an example of what I wrote:

> *The next question Jean asks me is "Sherry, I don't understand why getting started writing is so difficult. Tell me why it is." "Jean, one of the reasons that getting started is difficult is because. . . ."*

Taking my writing back to the conversational level helped me to focus on one person and one believable question, and got me rolling.

☐ MINDMAPPING

The biggest complaint about writing is that it takes too much time. A useful technique for writing faster is mindmapping. Mindmapping is brainstorming on paper. When you are not clear about your point of view, mindmapping is an excellent way to discover your ideas. This writing technique also helps you organize your ideas and is excellent for speeding up the process of getting started. Many people who have studied writing say that this technique is the single most useful approach to writing they have ever used.

How does mindmapping clarify your thinking? You throw out a smorgasbord of ideas to ensure that none is left unexplored. You spread out your ideas in their full range and variation. You can then select the ones that are right for your memo and can decide how you want to organize them.

Mindmapping simulates how your ideas hit you; it maps the way your thoughts flow. When you finish a mind map, you can see your ideas for what they truly are: spontaneous bursts.

How do you start out? You write down your first thought, which acts like a cog, triggering connected throughts. As you're writing, interesting shapes emerge and spill over the page. Thoughts explode out into the corners without any seeming logic. One word sparks many other words and triggers new thoughts.

The final form is different for each person. A mind map can look like an array of balloons, clouds, circles, triangles, rectangles, arrows, or globs of encircled words. Some mind maps look like rivers with tributaries, others like branches sprouting from a tree, others like formations of a root system or spokes of a wheel. Here are two examples of mind maps actually composed by business managers.

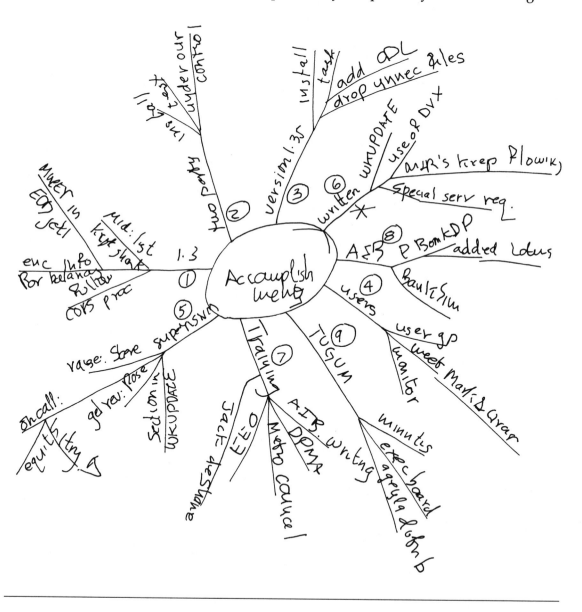

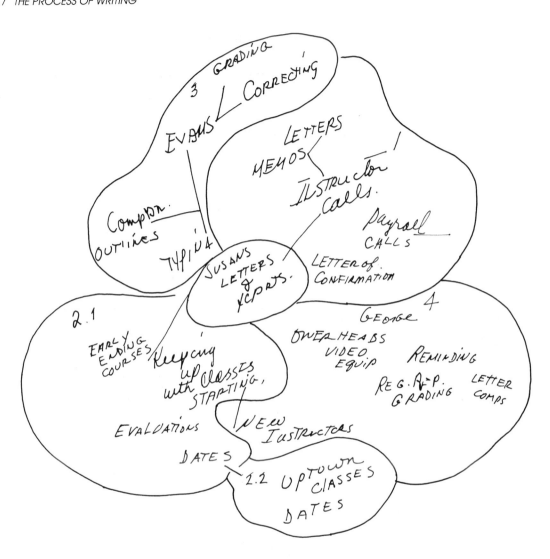

Why Mindmapping Is So Popular

1. Mindmapping Keeps Pace with Your Thoughts

Mindmapping eliminates the problem of your pencil not being able to keep up with the speed of your mind. Hands seem to move like sludge compared with thoughts; important ideas are lost. With mindmapping you can capture all your thoughts without losing any of them.

2. You Don't Have to Worry about Being Logical

Mindmapping frees you from worrying about ordering your ideas logically. Your goal is to uncover ideas, not to strive for order and coherence. The opposite is true when we begin writing with sentences and paragraphs. We are concerned that the first sentence flow logically and naturally into the second sentence. This over-concern with order slows down our writing speed and inhibits us.

3. You Unbury Your Creative Thoughts

Some of our richest ideas are often buried under the rubble of our initial, obvious thoughts. We have many more ideas than we think we do. When we write in sentences, we often make the first idea that strikes us the most important idea (because it came up first). We faithfully and deliberately stay on track with that idea, often eliminating the possibility of new ideas.

4. You Get a Bonus—An Outline of Your Ideas

Mindmapping is a playful, quick, and effortless way to outline. You don't have to grapple with following the form of a traditional, structured outline.

5. You Get a "Big Picture" View of Your Ideas

When your mind map is finished, you can see your thoughts all at once. With sentence-writing it is almost impossible to glance at a page of sentences and paragraphs and get an overview of the whole piece. You have to read each word, phrase, and sentence. You get stuck in the mire of the "little words," rather than seeing the big picture.

6. A Mind Map Isn't "Written in Stone"

Mindmapping doesn't intimidate people, because the outcome isn't permanent. It is only a preliminary step for collecting thoughts. This takes the psychological pressure off; you don't have to "get it right" immediately.

7. Mindmapping Only Takes a Few Minutes

By using this technique, you will reduce your overall writing time, because you will have clarified your thoughts prior to writing at the sentence level.

Procedure for Mindmapping

There's no right or wrong way for a mind map to look. No two mind maps will ever look alike. Some will have empty areas and others will be completely filled.

Step 1. *Take out an unlined piece of paper.* Why unlined? Lines infer rules and order. They constantly remind us: "Write on the line! Write left to right! The subject had better agree with the verb! Sentence 1 had better logically flow into sentence 2!" These rules stifle our creative thoughts. Lines force us into a straitjacket of orderliness.

Step 2. *Draw a circle two to three inches wide in the center of your paper.* (For many this is the most difficult part of mindmapping.) Why a circle? A circle does not infer order, right and wrong. It has no beginning, middle, or end. All points on the circle are equal, no one is more important than another. Ideas just exist, without ranking of importance, of which is first or last or best.

Step 3. *In the center of the circle, write down the subject of the memo you must write.*

Step 4. *Write down the first idea that hits your mind, triggered by the subject in the center of the circle.* This thought will be a cog or trigger for following thoughts. Where you place your ideas on the page doesn't matter. You can go to any corner or area of the page. Ideas can emanate from the circle or can be connected to each other by lines or arrows. It all depends on how they are associated.

Step 5. *Draw a line out from the circle to the idea you just wrote down.* (This will help you see how ideas are connected.) You can start at any point on the circle.

Step 6. *Enclose that idea in a circle, or, if you like, leave it as is.*

Step 7. *Write down the next new thought triggered by idea 1.* Then continue writing down succeeding thoughts. (Write in clipped phrases, using only nouns, verbs, adjectives. Just jot down the *kernel* of each idea.) You'll see that one idea trips off another. It's like the domino effect. Continue this process until you cannot think of any more ideas or associations.

Step 8. *If you get stuck on what to write next, go back to the center of the circle and study the subject.* Or look at the whole map and see if any new ideas come to mind.

Step 9. *Organize your ideas.* Once you have finished your mindmap, go back and organize it. Assign priorities to your ideas. When you finish, you will have a ready-made outline. It is an organized, bare-bones structure of your kernal thoughts.

Step 10. *Categorize your ideas.* Pull together groups of similar thoughts by using a lettering system (1a, 1b, 1c, 2a, 2b, 2c, etc.) or a color-coding system in which all similar ideas are encircled in one color.

You now have an even more fully developed outline! You are ready for the next stage of writing: sentences and paragraphs.

Ways to Use Mindmapping

You can use a mind map in all areas of your life, both personal and professional. On your job you can use it for (1) an outline for your next memo, letter, report, or proposal, (2) problem solving, (3) making notes prior to using a dictating machine, (4) project planning, (5) performance appraisal, (6) "to do" lists, (7) agendas for meetings, (8) a tough phone call or a tough verbal business communication, and/or (9) brainstorming for what word to use.

In your personal life, mindmapping can help you (1) clarify your personal goals and career goals, (2) solve a personal problem, (3) outline a difficult personal communication with a friend or spouse or child, and (4) make personal "to do" lists.

Teach your children to use mindmapping. The technique is a great way for kids to figure out their thoughts, too. It's especially helpful for kids who don't like to write.

☐ FREEWRITING

This writing technique will help you reach your number one objective as a writer: to put sentences on paper. In freewriting you write "stream of consciousness," that is, just the way you think. The trick is that you don't judge yourself while you're writing. You just write. The goal is to put as many words as possible on paper and *later* to edit those words with a critical eye.

Freewriting is like having dinner with a good friend. Your friend asks you a simple question about yourself and—zoom—you take off, talking on and on and on without censoring your thoughts or choice of words. Your thoughts are lucid, creative, and powerful. Before you know it, two hours have flown by. The reason this happens is that you are in an environment of acceptance. You feel trusting and free from judgment.

Let's take the opposite situation. Let's say you've been invited to dinner by your manager. You are very concerned about making a good impression. At dinner, you aren't yourself—your words come out unnatural and stilted. You want to sound interesting and well informed. You're worried about having good social graces—you agonize over exactly *when* to pick up your napkin and *which* spoon to use. Every minute seems like an eternity. You can hardly wait to get back home and be with people you feel comfortable around.

When you write, you can create either of these two situations in your head. You can either be your own best friend or your manager. *You* are responsible for creating the environment in which you write.

Following is an example of a "freewrite" on being concise that I first drafted for this book. It probably will make very little sense to you. It took me three minutes sitting at the word processor, with my eyes closed so I wouldn't be tempted to read or judge what I was writing. During the process I discovered a new principle. Look at how I ignored errors in spelling and incomplete thoughts and just concentrated on creating ideas, not editing them. Notice, too, how the writing flows naturally from thought to thought, just the way the mind works.

Freewriting Example

art of being concise includes the assujmption that you are at the same time being complete. being complete is assumed in the defifintio of being cohncise. my god, I think i have a new principle, after all these years. help. the principle is, be comletre. p i can't even spell it. be complete. you have to decide what is complete or not complete. you have to decide how much information to include or not to include in the conent. complete is conetent, concise in the number of words. people are so concise, they are incomplete in their words, and in their content. In fact, being concise has to do with writing what is necessary. It's not just concentrating on what is unnecessary. It's length, it's shortness, is irrelevant.

A more comprehensive definition of concise then is to decide what is necessary in content and in words, and then get rid of unnecessary words. Deciding what is necessary is the tough part of being concise. It means using just the right amount of

Here is my edit of this freewrite. It took me about four minutes to complete.

An Edited Freewrite

The standard definition of concise is "using no unnecessary words." (This definition comes from the writer's Bible, Strunk and White's *Elements of Style*.) This definition needs to be expanded because many people interpret it as meaning, "Be short and sweet." Unfortunately, they are so short and sweet that they are abrupt in tone or incomplete in information.

Part of being concise includes also being complete. It means not just crossing out unnecessary words; it means deciding what content and information to include in the first place. The foundation of being concise is that you must have the right amount of information and content to begin with before you are ready to delete unnecessary words.

The Benefits of Freewriting

1. You Will Write Two to Three Times Faster

Most people say it would normally take them double or triple the time to come up with the core of good ideas that they uncover when they freewrite. Much of that time would be spent in searching for the right word, procrastinating, or staring at a blank page. Usually you can use a third to a half of what you freewrite in your final piece. Even though you have to throw some things away, you have words on paper, and that is the point. What you have will have been written quickly and effortlessly because you will be going *along with* your ideas rather than *against* them.

2. You Will Be Prepared for Your Next Stage of Writing: Editing

Freewriting propels you into the editing stage. After you freewrite, you have sentences and paragraphs. You have something to work from. One of the toughest parts of writing is creating something from nothing. Freewriting gets you over that hurdle.

3. You Will Write More Creatively

You will find that your stream of consciousness uncovers authentic and colorful ways of communicating. You will find unconventional words, phrases, and ideas that are expressed so well they grab the reader's interest.

4. You Will Write More Honestly

You will be more yourself when you freewrite, because you're following your inner voice. There will be less of a split between the "real you" and the "business-writing you."

How to Freewrite

Step 1. *Set up a ten- to twenty- minute time limit.* Plan a block of private, undistracted writing time, with limits so that it won't seem like an endless task. Ten minutes is a good length of time, because it will seem that you can quit soon and reward yourself.

Step 2. *Write, write, write!* When you freewrite, you write for yourself and no one else. This is a chance to go into detail about your point of view. Forget what anyone else might think. The goal is to figure out what you think, and how you want to say it. Let your ideas fly! Let your mind flow like a stream. Write down as much as you can of what comes to mind even if the thoughts don't make sense and are not whole sentences. Every word that you write is part of a kernel thought and has value. Ignore spelling errors. (You will edit them out later.)

Why does writing stream of consciousness seem strange? Because it's writing without judgment, which is a new experience. We often stop while we're writing in the traditional way because we're criticizing, judging, editing ourselves as we write. A battle is going on in our head between our creative side and our judgmental side. The judgmental side is run by a character I call the "critical judge." Often our judgments can paralyze us so that writing comes to a complete standstill.

Another reason that writing without stopping is difficult is because we allow ourselves to be edited by the voices of those who influence us—our manager, the reader—and voices from past teachers (reminding us to be correct!). We are influenced to the point that we ignore our original thought (the one we should write down while we're freewriting). We slam breaks on our initial words and then edit, reword, and rephrase them. Finally, what we write doesn't even vaguely resemble our first words; often it is an overedited, less effective version. The following is typically what happens to us. For example, if the fellow in the following cartoon had been freewriting, he would have written down his first words: "John, please send me your recommendations . . .", instead of editing his original words and ending up with jargony, boring ones.

Step 3. *If you get stuck on where to start freewriting, try these two start-up methods:*

1.   The Basic Warm-up Method. In your first paragraph, write about your surroundings or whatever related or unrelated business thoughts are on your mind. This will break down your resistance and get you involved and started. For example:

> *It's 4:22:06 and it's raining outside and I don't want to get stuck in the rain. I forgot my umbrella and I wish I weren't sitting here and I guess I'd better get started with Maryann's performance appraisal. Her strengths are . . ."*

You will find that simply moving your pencil across the paper is reinforcing movement that gets you started and helps you get involved.

2.   The Mark Doty Heart-to-Heart Method.* In this method you write down emotional issues that are on your mind. If you're angry about some situation, write about it. The psychological theory is that writing it down makes it disappear, or at least clears the way for getting on with the business at hand.

---

*Mark Doty is a teenage friend of mine from Colorado.

Here is an example of writing from the heart, done by Mark when he was 8 years old. He was unhappy with a column in a children's magazine and told the editor exactly what he thought.

Dear Obnoxio
I hate your column.
It is junk and trash
I got the address and burned
the issue.
You are a totlae jerk
M.D

Obviously you can't write this honestly in business. But until you get past your true feelings, anger or whatever, you won't be able to communicate constructively. Writing can take the lid off the volcano. Writing down your feelings helps you move out of negative feelings and break through into acceptable solutions and language. The following is how the method could be used in business.

My boss is making me write this and I really resent it. I know I won't be able to sign my name to it. I hate ghost writing. Anyway, I'm writing whatever is on my mind. Now, the reason we need to purchase 20 new word processors is. . . .

(Of course privacy is essential when you're freewriting!)

Step 4. ***If you get stuck in the middle of your freewrite, try the Summarizing Method.*** If you can't remember where you've been and where you're going with your ideas, try this: Summarize, in writing, the subject or flow of thoughts you have been writing about prior to getting stuck. For example: "So, let me summarize. What I've been saying is that we have to purchase 20 new word processors . . . ." This usually gets you back on track and clicks you into your next thought. Your summary statement often becomes a succinct version of what you've been trying to say (and you may be able to frontload the words later!).

Step 5. *Acknowledge any criticisms you hear running through your mind.* There are times when your "critical judge" and the voices of others will needle you. You have two choices: (1) Be aware of the criticisms, but don't let them influence your writing and try to move back into your writing again or (2) Write down exactly what the criticisms are. The important thing is to realize that the criticisms exist and that they are interrupting your flow of thoughts.

Step 6. *Be aware of the physical signs of self-criticism.* Observe your behavior. These are the telltale signs that you are criticizing your own writing:

- Erasing
- Crossing out words
- Throwing away your paper
- Daydreaming
- Going to the dictionary or thesaurus
- Stopping to correct spelling, punctuation, or grammar
- Rereading constantly

Step 7. *Continue writing until you've exhausted your ideas.* Now you are ready for the easier part of the writing process—editing.

Reservations about Freewriting

Some people complain that with freewriting they have too many unnecessary words to edit, too much dead language to get rid of. To a certain degree, this is a valid point. However, until you have words on paper, you have only thoughts floating through your mind, and thoughts don't count. Written words count.

Further, what may seem like a worthless word at the time ("worthless" is itself a criticism!) may eventually lead into a paragraph, theme, or solution to a problem. Even the extra words you decide to edit out served a purpose: They catapulted you into fuller thoughts.

□ A FASTER PROCESS OF WRITING

If you think you write too slowly, or if you find writing a chore, you have nothing to lose in trying a new process of writing. You need to find a process that suits your style, and then you can use variations of it every time you write.

Typically, when we write *we try to do too many things at once.* We overload ourselves because we try to create, write, organize, and

edit all at the same time. Here are all the things we try to do at once: Figure out what we think—come up with workable ideas—attach words to the pictures in our mind—make sure the ideas flow logically—consider the reader's reactions—spell perfectly—check our handwriting to make sure it's legible—watch for correct grammar—remember the fleeting thoughts that whiz by while we continue to write on the same idea—edit so the first draft will be near perfect!—and much more! The rule is, *if you try to do too many things at once, you do none of them well.* It's like trying to keep four plates twirling in the air all at once.

Mindmapping and freewriting are two new strategies to add to your repertoire for a new process of writing. A combination of the two into such a process might look like this:

When you use mindmapping and freewriting, look at how much more efficient you are with your writing time.

Old Process	Time	New Process	Time
Procrastination	15	Mindmap	5
Blank-page panic	5	Organize mindmap	5
Write and edit in head at same time	30	Freewrite	10
Edit	10	Edit	15
Total: 60 minutes		Total: 35 minutes	

You have saved 35 minutes of writing and thinking time. And I'll bet you've written a more effective memo, too.

Strategies for a Faster Process of Writing

1. Start Writing Sooner

The sooner you start writing, the better your writing will be, because you will have more time to edit your work. This means spending less time procrastinating.

2. Take One Step at a Time

Break your writing into segments. In other words, don't try to create, write, organize, and edit all at the same time, but separate the process of writing into different stages.

6

The Editing Process

The last phase of the writing process is editing. Editing can turn a mediocre piece into a masterpiece. It can change a confusing message into a coherent one.

All communication is a constant process of editing. We forever change, expand on, and rearrange our thoughts and words so we can maximize our chances of being heard and understood. The only difference between editing when we speak and editing when we write is that in the first we edit *while* we're speaking.

Editing threatens us less than writing because the stress of the creative process is gone. We are working with the known: words on paper. It's safer inside the world of black-print-on-paper than it is inside the world of unwritten, invisible, unpredictable thoughts.

You can eliminate the editing process if you know exactly what you want to say and how you want to say it, or if you've said it a hundred times before. That doesn't happen very often, however; most communications are unique between you and someone else. The words have to be mulled over and worked out.

□ THE BENEFITS OF EDITING

Editing sharpens our precision as communicators. It gives us more control over our message and over what our readers read. The invaluable part about the editing phase is that it takes us outside of ourselves so that we start looking at our communications through new eyes—the eyes of the reader.

□ WHY IS EDITING OUR OWN WRITING SO TOUGH?

Editing means no longer having things our own way. In editing we must put our writing selves aside and become subservient to our reader and to our message. We must let our reader's needs take over.

Editing also means making decisions. We must think rigorously, deciding what to throw away, how to organize ideas, and which words to choose so that our writing will be the best it can be. Saying good-bye to our words is hard, especially if we've struggled to find the right ones.

□ EDITING STRATEGIES

1. Type Your Drafts

It's hard to take your writing seriously until it's typed. When your words are typed, you can focus on your ideas rather than trying to decipher your handwriting. You can also get an idea of the design for the final layout.

2. Take Breaks

You read your writing more objectively when you take breaks. Without breaks, you have blind spots because you put meaning where it may not be. Your mind is thinking along one groove and your emotions are filling in the gaps and compensating for missing information. You see a partial, distorted picture—your writer's picture.

Why do minds and emotions invent things that aren't there? When you've written down your ideas, you've put your head and heart into your work, and how could you hope to be objective? Your words are a part of you. But you need to cut the cord that binds them to you, and taking a break makes that easier.

A short break is better than no break at all. However, the more time you can put between you and your writing, the better. Just make sure your breaks aren't so long that you lose interest or begin building up resistance to the editing process.

Here are some general suggestions for editing.

- Give one third of your words to Goodwill.
- Underline critical points and frontload them.
- Identify major subjects and give each subject a separate paragraph.
- Add titles and headings for easier reading.

☐ GIVING YOUR MEMO A "TEST RUN"

1. Read Out Loud What You've Written

Your own voice is your most reliable editor. What your eyes won't tell you, your ears will. The spoken editorial voice automatically makes changes in words, punctuation, and phrasing, and awkward areas become noticeable. Reading out loud works because you use additional sensory channels: your ears, vocal cords, mouth, and tongue. Your voice takes writing back to its source—your speech.

Ernest Hemingway believed in the technique of editing by reading out loud. That is how he checked for clarity and beauty of language. Before publishing it, he read *The Old Man and the Sea* aloud several hundred times to guide him in his editorial changes. This technique explains why his style is natural and easy to read. He believed in the concept that writing is speaking on paper.

2. Set Up a Formal "Editing Buddy System"

Find someone in your office who is willing to make a formal agreement to exchange editorial comments. That person should be someone you feel comfortable with, someone whose opinion you respect, and someone you don't have to impress.

Ask for short, five-minute feedback sessions; don't make a big production out of what you want your editor to do. All you're asking for is an honest, brief reaction to your words and message. If you make a big thing out of someone being your editor, you may get turned down. Some people resent being asked for too much of their time, and others don't feel competent to be "an editor."

3. Use Good Secretaries

A good secretary is one of the best untapped resources for editorial feedback. She (or he) comes to the page with a fresh, less political viewpoint. When you ask your secretary to check for clarity, don't tell her what you're trying to communicate. That's cheating. Allow *her* to tell *you* what she thinks you're trying to communicate. Then you will honestly know if you've made your point.

One head of an entire training division at IBM says she always passes her memos by her secretary before she sends them out. Her philosophy is that if her secretary can't understand it, she has failed to communicate clearly.

There are two payoffs for using your secretary as an editor:

1. **Your Secretary Will Feel Acknowledged.** Asking for editorial comments is an acknowledgment of your secretary's good judgment and ability to think. Why? Because editing is a high-level thinking skill, not a routine one like proofreading.

2. **Your Secretary's Typing Speed and Accuracy Will Increase.** Your secretary will no longer be typing mechanically but will see the larger picture and the larger issues. Typing accuracy and speed naturally increase when the overall picture and meaning are clear.

4. Proofread Your Work Before You Send It

A solid policy to follow is that you should *always* reread the final copy before you send it. The one time you don't, there's sure to be an error. Here's an example of a memo that a manager forgot to proofread (imagine his embarrassment).

MEMO

To: Cynthia Heim

From: T.J. Mallon

Subject: Plans, Problems, Accomplishments (Lunch)

I take great pleasure in inviting you and your managers to meet with Shirley Rickord and to review and eat the above subject.

Time: 10:30
Place: 5028 Wentworth
Date: July 6

☐ HOW TO BE A BETTER EDITOR

When people ask you to edit their work for them, follow these suggestions on how to be an effective editor.

The Six Do's of Editing

1. **DO** use positive, nonjudgmental language, letting the writer know if his memo—

   - Is effective or ineffective.
   - Works or doesn't work.
   - Achieves its goal or doesn't achieve its goal.
   - Creates action or doesn't create action.
   - Persuades or doesn't persuade.

2. **DO** comment on clarity and organization.
3. **DO** be specific and comment on individual words, sentences, and paragraphs.
4. **DO** listen to your inner voice as a guide for your editorial comments.
5. **DO** use "I" messages versus "you" messages. For example, say—

- "I'm confused," rather than "you're confusing."
- "I'm unclear," rather than "you are being unclear."

6. **DO** use positive feedback on which memos are effective and why. For example:

- "This is very clear."
- "I feel important here."
- "Good purpose statement."

The Four Don'ts of Editing

1. **DON'T** use vague editing jargon. For example:

- "This needs to be more clear and concise."
- "Needs a different style."

2. **DON'T** use negative, judgmental editorial language, telling the writer his memo is . . .

- Good or bad.
- Right or wrong.

3. **DON'T** comment on *just* spelling, punctuation, and grammar.
4. **DON'T** use a red pencil for corrections (it has negative associations).

☐ HOW TO MAKE THE MOST OF BEING EDITED

There are times when you will be edited by someone else. Always keep in mind the advantages of getting editorial feedback:

1. You Receive Useful Information about How You Are Being Perceived

When else in business and in life can you get open reactions to the way you are communicating? Editorial feedback is invaluable for this reason alone. You don't have to agree with the comments, but at least you have an idea about what one person "heard" when he or she read your writing.

2. You Are Forced to Define Your Philosophy of Communication and Writing

Your editor's comments will challenge you to communicate more effectively. They will confirm whether you are successfully applying your philosophy of communication.

3. You Will Learn Much about Your Editor

If your editor is your manager, this is a golden opportunity to find out more about him or her. You can learn more about his or her philosophy of communications and stance on company politics.

☐ HOW TO HAVE EFFECTIVE EDITING SESSIONS

Here are some suggestions on how to use editing sessions productively.

1. Avoid the Trap of Debating and Philosophizing about "Good" Writing

Editing sessions can turn into philosophical debates that lead to nowhere when people talk about writing "in general." Remember, the real issue with regard to effective writing is not so much what anyone's general points of view are but how an individual responds as a reader to one particular memo.

2. Ask for Specific Editorial Comments Rather than "Editorialese"

Ask your editor to *circle the words* that create a positive or negative reaction. Unfortunately, many people resort to "editorialese," such as "I think you need to rework this memo so it is more clear and concise." This is not helpful, because it is vague. It's much more helpful to hear from an editor: "I'm confused by this word," or "This idea is already known to your reader." *That* is specific feedback.

3. Ask Specific Questions about Your Writing

Lead your editor if he or she doesn't know how to give specific feedback. The following are questions you can ask to help you get more specific reactions.

1. Is my style appropriate for my reader?
2. Which words are too formal/informal, impersonal/personal, forceful/weak, routine/colorful?
3. Is my content too broad or too detailed?
4. Is the organization of the ideas clear? If not, where specifically not?
5. Is critical information highlighted?

4. Stand Up for Your Point of View

Some writers assume that they have no right to speak up if an editor or senior person edits their work. They may get overedited because they take editorial comments in silence. If you come across a particular editorial comment that you don't agree with and feel strongly about, speak up. But when you do, be sure to justify why you wrote it that way. The words you could use might sound something like this, "I placed this paragraph third instead of second because the reader needs to be eased into the negative message. This way it isn't a slap in the face." Your explanation will prove that you went through a careful thinking process and will make it less easy for the editor to disagree with you.

5. Don't Argue over Trivia

Don't quibble and nitpick over every last editorial comment. What's the use 'of disagreeing over things that don't make a big difference—a word here or a minor writing point there in less important memos? It isn't worth your time and effort.

Your goal should be to help win the war for improved communication rather than to win minor sideshow battles. What's worth battling for? Writing skills that make a difference, that do the following:

• Provide a complete, clear message so that no extra phone calls or additional communications are needed

- Improve response time to requests
- Make your memos get read
- Make your reader receive your negative message in a positive way
- Prove the credibility of you and your business

☐ THINGS TO REMEMBER IF YOU'RE BEING OVEREDITED

Sometimes people are overedited by their managers or by company editors. When this happens to you, maintain your perspective and remember:

1. You are not your writing. Separate yourself from it. Your writing is only one limited part of you.
2. This is just one reaction to one piece of writing. A different person would have a different response.
3. You're never a perfect verbal communicator, so why expect yourself to be one-hundred-percent perfect as a written communicator?

If you feel you are being overedited by your manager, you need to determine why. The first step is to find out what your manager is reacting to. Is it the content and thrust of your ideas, or the clarity, or the organization? If it is the content, then the two of you need to sit down and discuss the ideas so that you can come to an agreement. If the editorial comments center on clarity and organization, you need specific reactions from your manager.

Here are some questions to ask yourself to help you decide why your writing is being overedited.

- In general, is writing a skill I need to work on?
- Is my manager personally interested in developing my written communication skills?
- Is my manager working to establish group writing standards?
- Is my manager working to establish department credibility?

- Are these high-risk memos?
- Are the readers critical players in my business group?
- Has my writing become an arena for deciding who is managing?
- Am I competing over who has superior business competence?
- Am I and my manager competing over who has a superior educational and social background?

Editorial discussions are sometimes smokescreens for personality differences. If you and your manager do have personality differences, realize that the words you're arguing over aren't the real issue. The printed word is often used as a battleground because it's a tangible bone to gnaw on. The real issue is the personality difference. You need to deal with the real problem and put the editorial comments in their proper perspective.

If you determine that you are being overedited because of a concern for helping you develop your writing style, here are three things you can do to have more productive sessions.

1. Study your manager/editor's writing style. Your manager has a distinctive written communication style. Keep a file with examples of his or her writing and study that style.

Look for common ground and for differences in your writing styles. Does your manager tend to write in detail and cover all the bases, or to write "net"? Is his or her style flexible depending on the reader, or is it fairly consistent? Are bullets used? Are the words formal or informal? What seem to be the favorite words?

Select the parts of your manager's writing style that are new to you and experiment with them. Then decide if you feel comfortable using them, and if they are effective when you use them.

2. Read the same books and take the same workshops on communication. Work toward finding books and experts on effective communication and writing that you both respect. Outside experts can help clarify issues and defuse arguments. By reading and listening to the same experts, you can begin to use a common business-writing language and have common ground to work from. You can then use a mutual language (such as, "Let's frontload this purpose statement") without confusing each other.

Request group training sessions for persuasive business writing. Few corporations have in-house trainers who are writing consultants—writing is a highly technical skill and few people feel at ease with their skill, even trainers with PhD's. Most corporations thus hire outside writing consultants to conduct training courses.

3. Write two versions of the same memo—your manager's and yours. Don't identify which version is whose, and then ask someone you both respect to react to both.

7

Maintaining a Positive Attitude toward Writing

Everything in life boils down to one thing: attitude. This chapter will show you how to maintain or develop a positive attitude about writing. It discusses:

1. Training yourself to be an effective communicator
2. Managing your writing time
3. Creating the right environment
4. Dealing with the "I want to be perfect" syndrome
5. Keeping writing in perspective
6. Reminding yourself of the rewards

☐ TRAINING YOURSELF TO BE AN EFFECTIVE COMMUNICATOR

Learning communication skills is like learning anything else. Formal study is not necessary. What is necessary is the motivation to learn. Some people go to school and formally study the fields of communications, advertising, linguistics, journalism, languages, and English. Others take practical communications courses or read how-to books.

Most people study communications informally. They consciously observe events around them. They are not just participants in or victims of the communication process; they try to understand what is going on when people talk to each other. They have power because they play two roles: the role of participator and the role of observer.

The following suggestions will help you improve your general communication skills.

1. Become an Observer of Communications, Not Just a Participator

Learn to step back and observe what is going on in a communication rather than being in the thick of it. Your goal is to play the two roles of communicator and observer. Your observations will bring you new awareness about yourself and others.

Start reading business memos, letters, reports, and proposals more analytically. Notice what other business writers do that either retains your interest or bores you.

2. Study the Expert Communicators

Study what the experts do to grab and maintain your interest. What does President Reagan say and how does he say it that he has won the title "the great communicator"?

Study advertisers. Actively watch TV commercials and read magazine ads. You will begin to notice why one piece of junk mail catches your eye while another doesn't. You will be not just a consumer of information but an analyst as well.

3. Study Street Communications

Become a spectator in the sport of sidewalk communications. Whenever a person opens his or her mouth it is an opportunity for you to learn about how people communicate. Listen carefully when interesting communications go on between bus drivers and riders, waiters and customers, and so on.

4. Study Yourself

Use your life as a communications lab. The art of communication is a lifelong study and pursuit. (Anyone who has had marriage counseling or therapy will tell you that.) Your interest in writing will spill over into all areas of your life—reading, speaking, listening.

The best place to start learning anything about society is yourself. You must observe how you communicate with others, in your personal and professional life. You must recall and analyze your successful communications as well as your troublesome, unsuccessful communications. And, as an additional fascinating study, you can observe how you communicate privately with yourself in all situations.

What do effective writers do when they write? How do recognized religious leaders gain a following? Which of your friends is an especially effective communicator, and why? Use all the resources around you.

☐ MANAGING YOUR TIME

Writing takes time. You will never find the kind of time and space you need to write until you start treating writing as a time-management issue.

Setting Priorities

You alone decide what kind of priority writing has in your life—not your manager, some trainer, or your reader. No one else can convince you of the importance of writing. This is your decision. When people decide that certain behavior is important to their lives, they act. If you are convinced that writing is a critical skill you need for your success, you will find time to write. Your conviction will call the shots as to how you organize your time.

What's the Right Time?

1. Write during Your "Prime Time"
This is your best thinking time and it differs for each person. For many it's the early part of the day. However, some people say that they write best when they are tired, because then they are less apt to judge themselves. You must decide for yourself.

2. Write in Chunks of Time

Write in blocks of at least fifteen to twenty minutes. That way you can concentrate better and get more involved with your writing.

3. Write during "Clean Mental Slate" Times

Select times when you can concentrate. Times when you have lots of things on your mind are not good times to write. Clean up the details and concerns that crowd your thoughts so that you can approach your writing with a clear mind. If things keep popping into your head while you're writing, write down those items on a nearby "to do" list.

Dealing with the No-Time-to-Write Problem

Here is how some people solve the problem of having no time to write.

1. They Willfully Create Time to Write

People create blocks of writing time and then delegate tasks, to make this time their own. They set up new procedures and responsibilities so that their support staff is responsible for the lower priority tasks that interrupt writing time.

2. They Write at Home on Workdays

Some companies encourage their people to stay home and write. Is that possible in your company? Why not ask?

3. They Ask Management to Support Them in Creating Company Time for Writing

If you have to write consistently on your personal time (during lunch and at night) and you resent it, you need to work on changing the situation. If management expects you to write between 9:00 a.m. and 5:00 p.m. and it's impossible for you to do so, it's reasonable for you to request that management shift your work load temporarily or permanently. Management should be eager to help you succeed. When you succeed, the company succeeds. The key is to speak up.

Often management doesn't know you have a conflict about writing on personal time. So how can it fix the problem?

☐ CREATING THE RIGHT ENVIRONMENT

Each person has a personal preference as to what perfect writing conditions are. Always strive for the conditions right for you, because then you can write at your best.

Obviously, conditions are rarely ideal, especially with the typical pressure of business. Your goal is to be aware of the right conditions and to try consciously to create them. They are:

1. The Right Space

If you can't think clearly, you can't write. So find a place where you can concentrate. The ideal, of course, is to have a quiet place to write. However, some people have learned to concentrate in the midst of noise or chaos (look at newspaper reporters).

You should also have a sense of privacy. Find a place where you feel no one is peering over your shoulder. (And when you finish, file your writing away where no one will see it until you're ready to share it.) Try:

- Your office (put your phone on call forwarding and a *Do Not Disturb* sign on your door)
- The company library
- The conference room
- An empty office

Other suggestions:

- Request that your secretary not interrupt you until a certain time.
- Tell people you are writing—they will respect your need for seclusion.
- Tell people the hours you are available so they will know when you are accessible.

2. The Right Physical Comfort

You must make yourself as physically comfortable as possible (within reasonable limits, of course!) For some writers, this means loosening the tie or taking off shoes.

3. The Right Diet

A diet of caffeine and sugar prevents people from concentrating. Eating and drinking nutritious foods increase your ability to concentrate while you write.

4. The Right Writing Tools

Have your favorite writing tools on hand when you write. Until I started using a word processor, I felt ready to write only when I had my favorite black-and-silver mechanical pencil and thin-lined legal-size pads.

☐ DEALING WITH THE "I WANT TO BE PERFECT" SYNDROME

If you give one-hundred percent of your effort to your writing and write from the heart, the result will be good enough, even if you feel you didn't find exactly the right words. The important thing is that you write out of honesty and conviction.

People accept each other's imperfections when their communications are founded in honesty. It is when people write to impress or to control situations that their imperfections glare at the reader.

Once you accept that your writing will never be perfect, but that what you do will be good enough, you'll be able to write more freely.

☐ KEEPING WRITING IN PERSPECTIVE

When you start to worry about a particular writing task because of your fear of criticism, you need to reassess your perspective and then fit writing into the larger picture. Remember:

1. Each Memo You Write Is a Grain of Sand in the Whole Scheme of Things

We take our memos too seriously. One memo is not going to change our lives or our readers' lives, perfect or imperfect, mistake or no mistake.

Let's look at how insignificant even big events can be. Can you remember who won the pole vault in the 1984 U.S. Summer Olympics? Probably not. The event was shown on international TV, and millions watched. Yet very, very few can remember who won.* So what makes us think that one memo is going to make *that* much difference?

2. The "Paper You" Is Not the Real You

We get confused into thinking that *we* are our writing. It isn't true. Our writing is only a representation of us. We are far more important than any memo could ever be.

3. Compare Yourself Only with Yourself

Comparing yourself with others undermines your self-confidence. The important thing is that you look at where you've been in your attitude and experience with writing, and see how far you've come and how far you want to go. When you find yourself worrying about how your CEO would write it, remember that all of us write in our own distinctive way.

☐ REMINDING YOURSELF OF THE REWARDS

1. You Will Learn to Accept Yourself More Fully

Accepting your writing is a way of accepting yourself. If you can begin to accept the perfect and imperfect forms of yourself that you find in your writing, you can begin to accept yourself more fully.

Your writing is a mirror that forces you to look at yourself and come to terms with yourself. If you look, this is what you will see:

---

*Pierre Quinon was the gold medalist.

- Where you feel confident or intimidated
- Where you have the courage to be direct and where you skirt real issues
- Where you abdicate original thinking to form thinking
- Where you are clear or unclear about what you think
- Where you use plain English to express yourself rather than fancy English to impress others

2. Writing Can Give You Self-Dignity, Self-Trust

If you believe in your distinctiveness, then writing becomes an act of self-trust, a symbol of self-dignity. By writing, you are confirming that you have a legitimate right to speak out. By communicating in a permanent form, you are saying, "I have something to say; I have value. This is the way I see the world."

3. Writing Will Help You Be Remembered

Studs Terkel wrote a book called *Working*. He interviewed hundreds of people to find out what motivated them to work, and what they liked and didn't like about their work. He found that the one desire everybody had in common, from corporate president to bricklayer to paper boy, was to be *remembered*. What better way to be remembered than to write!

4. Writing Will Help You Reach Your Potential

Your writing will be a testament to your commitment, to your determination to communicate despite your fear of being judged imperfect.

I wish for all of you that as a result of reading this book and practicing your writing, you will begin to see that you are communicating who you are more effectively on paper, and that you will begin to hear people comment:

"*Loved your last memo, Ted. You're beginning to find your own voice.*"

Drawing by Lorenz; © 1984 The New Yorker Magazine, Inc.

8

Exercises

This chapter consists of forty-two exercises that reinforce the material presented in this book. Work only on those exercises that meet your writing needs. The exercises cover four major writing areas:

- The principles of communication
- The principles of persuasion
- Selection of effective words
- Tone and style

Answers to the exercises appear on pages 216 to 227. The exercises are as follows:

The Principles of Communication (pages 177–195)

1. Identifying purposes of writing.
2. Clarifying your purpose for writing.
3. Identifying purpose statements in memos.
4. Rewriting purpose statements.

5. Using visual imagery as a clarity check.
6. Including a missing word.
7. Rephrasing disconnected thoughts.
8. Shortening long sentences.
9. Being explicit.
10. Being specific.
11. Columnizing numbers.
12. Eliminating redundant words in a sentence.
13. Shortening wordy expressions.
14. Eliminating unnecessary words in a sentence.
15. Eliminating "it" expressions.
16. Making a wordy letter concise.
17. Organizing sentences in a letter.
18. Organizing paragraphs.
19. Subject/verb agreement.
20. Using parallel structure in a sentence.
21. Using parallel structure in lists.
22. Using parallel structure in procedural memos.

The Principles of Persuasion (pages 195–203)

23. Getting to the point.
24. Ordering information according to the reader's interest.
25. Ordering achievements in a resume.
26. Frontloading in subject titles.
27. Frontloading in sentences.
28. Writing dynamic subject titles.
29. Using reference headings.
30. Burying "distractors."
31. Using follow-up statements.

Selection of Effective Words (pages 203–207)

32. Rewriting business jargon.
33. Rewriting routine endings.
34. Impressing versus expressing.
35. Using words that create visual images.

Tone and Style (pages 208–215)

36. Identifying the passive and active voices.
37. Changing the passive voice to active voice.
38. Changing the passive voice to active voice.
39. Recycling nouns into verbs.
40. Finding hidden verbs.
41. Converting negative tone to positive tone.
42. Final writing exercise: rewriting an ineffective letter.

☐ THE PRINCIPLES OF COMMUNICATION

Exercise 1: IDENTIFYING PURPOSES OF WRITING

Directions: Decide what the one *critical* purpose is for each of the following pieces. The purpose can be to (1) inform, (2) create action, or (3) entertain.

———   1. *The New York Times* newspaper

———   2. Advertisement for the "new Coke"

———   3. Two-hundred-word composition on "What I Did Last Summer"

———   4. Your last resume

Exercise 2: CLARIFYING YOUR PURPOSE FOR WRITING

Directions: Indicate if the following critical purpose statements are intended to inform (I), to request action (A), or to persuade (P). They can have two purposes.

_____ 1. For your information, listed below is the status of the items we discussed at the 4/5/83 meeting.

_____ 2. We need your approval to purchase an IBM typewriter.

_____ 3. This is just a brief memo to thank you for arranging the interview with Bruce Bergman.

_____ 4. This memo is to confirm our discussion regarding the problems associated with the exposure items on the domestic institutional banks and to outline recommendations.

_____ 5. You have expressed an interest in the possible purchase of First Bank of Minneapolis' Mohawk 2405-Series 21 System. I am submitting to you the specs of our present system and will describe the outstanding benefits of the Mohawk System.

_____ 6. Subject: Error Checks
Last year we had a problem keeping track of checks we should have received for various errors. This year the check process will be monitored in a different manner. Please follow the following procedures.

_____ 7. I propose that we hire an additional typist and will outline the benefits below.

_____ 8. I recommend that Sherwood Rudin be promoted to Lead Clerk for three reasons.

_____ 9. We have been getting feedback from branches that the New Savings Plan is not working.

_____ 10. Please submit two to three samples of your writing by June 8th to the following address: 417 19th Avenue South, Minneapolis, Minnesota 55419.

Exercise 3: IDENTIFYING PURPOSE STATEMENTS IN MEMOS

Directions: Underline the purpose statement in each of the following two memos. (The statement should be repositioned at the beginning of the memo.)

MEMO 1:

Subject: 931–07899

On September 4, 1985, client purchased $40m GNMA 13% of 5034. The pool factor was incorrectly calculated and confirmed to client creating $355 overcharge. The trading desk advised us to internally adjust the price and charge the account representative accordingly.

Please approve credit of $355 to account 931–07899; we will charge account representative #4165.

MEMO 2:

Subject: Approval to review candidates outside Westchester

Mike, attached please find a copy of a replacement requisition for Edward Jones. I have been searching the Westchester area for over three months for qualified candidates with a strong working knowledge of APL to support the Chemical Data System. Thus far I have been unsuccessful in finding candidates. As a result, the project is in jeopardy of missing deadlines that the CDS Staff consider vital to the success of the CDS project.

Therefore, I am requesting your support and assistance to obtain the approvals required to begin reviewing candidates from outside the Westchester area, and if necessary, from outside the firm.

Exercise 4: REWRITING PURPOSE STATEMENTS

Directions: The following memo has a buried purpose statement. Rewrite and frontload this statement.

Proposal: An Approach to Management Development at JPS

JPS's recent past reflects a renewed vitality and an upward trend in development and growth. Key ingredients behind this trend have been the management capabilities and work force. To sustain and enhance the accelerated growth which JPS has projected for itself over the next several years, a management development program is outlined.

Rewrite: (If you're stuck, start with, "The purpose of this proposal is . . .")

Exercise 5: USING VISUAL IMAGERY AS A CLARITY CHECK

Directions: Read the following sentences and observe whether the words create a clear picture in your mind or whether they create static or blankness. Check off only those sentences that create a picture.

_____ 1. For breakfast this morning I had the upper part of a hog's hind leg with two oval bodies encased in a shell laid by a female bird.

_____ 2. I had ham and eggs for breakfast this morning.

_____ 3. This is essential because of peak load work in new operations due to the assessment of the operating plan amendment.

———— 4. All the XYZ tapes listed below are in stock and are ready to ship within four hours.

———— 5. I could suggest a purification of departments within the function in order to approach an analysis to endeavor to clarify your requests.

Exercise 6: INCLUDING A MISSING WORD

Directions: The following memo announces two time management classes. As it is, you don't know if there are two 2-hour courses or one 4-hour course. Add one word to the first sentence to make it clear.

Subject: Enrollment for Time Management Classes

Two time management classes are scheduled to be presented by the Training Department. The classes will be held on Wednesday, March 30, and Wednesday, April 6, at 2:00 p.m. in Conference Room 2A. Classes will last approximately two hours.

The missing word is ————————.

Exercise 7: REPHRASING DISCONNECTED THOUGHTS

Directions: Rewrite the following unclear sentence.

Handling the callers and maintaining a professional and courteous attitude on the phone reflects to others how proud we are that you are part of our team.

Rewrite:

Exercise 8: SHORTENING LONG SENTENCES

Directions: Rewrite the following long, rambling sentences so that each sentence has only one idea.

1. I have two major "effective writing goals" and they are to organize my thoughts logically and to capture my reader's attention.

2. Christy Levin has enhanced my unit immeasurably because she has an ability to produce under stress and still maintain the quality of her work in addition to which she takes suggestions in a constructive manner.

3. Three weeks ago, a train bound for Manhattan from Queens broke down, stranding 1,500 passengers in a tunnel under the East River for more than an hour and concerned New York business people are banding together to lobby for change.

4. The dedication of the staff was above and beyond our expectations and was the ingredient that allowed on-time completion of the project despite computer failures and the late delivery of materials.

5. Carrie Jones reported a minor problem in her section and she assured me it will be corrected promptly—fortunately this has no effect on our balancing procedure.

Exercise 9: BEING EXPLICIT

Directions: The following general statements need more precise information. On the basis of your work experience, make the statements more concrete and provide specific details. For example:

Vague: A fair amount of work is involved in this task.
Specific: 142 auto parts need to be checked for quality control.

1. Please advise.

2. I would appreciate your attention to this matter.

3. His performance is not up to standard.

4. Call if you have any questions.

5. Productivity is up.

Exercise 10: BEING SPECIFIC

Directions: In each of the following sets, rank the words according to generality, labeling the most general word as 1.

1. _____ city

   _____ inhabited area

   _____ Minneapolis

2. _____ 298

   _____ lots

   _____ several dozen

3. _____ a human being.

   _____ staff writer

   _____ Sally Jones

   _____ a woman

   _____ staff

4. _____ the CPA program designer

   _____ Bob Barton

   _____ manager

   _____ the section manager

   _____ the entity

Exercise 11: COLUMNIZING NUMBERS

Directions: Categorize and create columns for the following stock information, which appeared in one section of a weekly highlight report.

Exxon Corp. #26984 400(s) since July 1986. Columns do not cross-foot. No reconciliation received.

Louisville Gas & El. #89624 400(s) since July 1986. Columns do not crossfoot. No reconciliation received.

NLT Corp. 52186 400(s) since June 1986. Code 6 rejected. Reconciliation received.

Rewrite:

**Exercise 12: ELIMINATING REDUNDANT WORDS IN A
SENTENCE**

Directions: Cross out the redundant words.

1. Thank you for your sincere and earnest efforts.

2. Your customers fall into numerous different categories.

3. These are the rules and regulations for security.

4. The ideas and concepts in this plan are excellent.

Exercise 13: SHORTENING WORDY EXPRESSIONS

Directions: Substitute one or two words for these wordy expressions.

1. during the course of _____
2. for the purpose of _____
3. in regard to _____
4. a week from next Monday _____
5. in the event that _____
6. we wish to thank you _____
7. in relation to _____
8. if you would be so kind as to _____
9. we must ask you to _____
10. at a later date _____
11. in view of the fact that _____
12. despite the fact that _____

Exercise 14: ELIMINATING UNNECESSARY WORDS IN A SENTENCE

Directions: Rewrite each sentence using fewer words to express the same thought. There are a variety of ways to streamline these sentences. Be creative.

1. Enclosed you will find your check in the amount of $29.95.

2. In view of the fact that the transactions will take place, would you be so kind as to prepare the data.

3. We have received your April 20 receipt, for which we most kindly thank you.

4. See Mr. Farren's memo that is attached which is a detailed discussion of the accounting issues.

5. Individuals and entities of outstanding talent and ability are given promotions by us.

6. In developing an annual budget for a finance company, two main considerations that play a key role in the budgeting process are (a) what are management's desired objectives and (b) are these objectives attainable.

7. If it will not be too much trouble, will you be kind enough to let us hear from you on or about the first of next month.

Exercise 15: ELIMINATING "IT" EXPRESSIONS

Directions: Omit the unnecessary "it" expressions and rewrite the sentence.

1. *It was a real pleasure* meeting with you and Christy Levin last Monday.

2. *It is my understanding that* you will discuss this with Cynthia Lewis.

3. *It has been brought to my attention that* some incoming phone calls are not being answered on a timely basis.

4. *It would be very much appreciated* if you could send us a new as-sessment of the property value.

5. *It is also interesting to note that* ABC Company has paid the French withholding tax on the highest amount.

6. *It is necessary* for you on Sunday to report early to power up all equipment.

Exercise 16: MAKING A WORDY LETTER CONCISE

Directions: Cross out the unnecessary words in this letter.

Subject: Identifying number

Dear Ms. Sweetnam:

It is required by the Internal Revenue Service that we supply them with Recipients' Identifying Number for those reportable on Form 1099 for the 1985 tax year.

To assist us in this regard, we would appreciate it if you would kindly insert your identifying number (Social Security number for an individual or identification number for an employer) and return this letter to us in the envelope provided.

Thank you for your cooperation and assistance.

Exercise 17: ORGANIZING SENTENCES IN A LETTER

Directions: The following is a letter requesting information on a trade transaction of XYZ stock. Number the sentences so they are in logical order.

July 13, 1985

Dear Ms. Gruber:

_____ 1. I am conducting a review of the transaction in the XYZ stock for the trade date May 15, 1985.

_____ 2. This request is made in accordance with Article IV, Section 5, of the Association's Rules of Fair Practice.

_____ 3. I need these documents by September 1, 1985.

_____ 4. On that date your firm executed two orders to sell 200 shares.

_____ 5. The purpose of this letter is to ask for your cooperation in helping my department review a trade transaction with your company.

_____ 6. If you have any questions, please feel free to contact me.

_____ 7. Please provide me with copies of these orders showing the times of execution.

Yours truly,
Beverly Hughes
Clearing Manager

Exercise 18: ORGANIZING PARAGRAPHS

Directions: The paragraphs in the following letter are scrambled. Unscramble them and number them according to their logical sequence.

Dear Mr. Blew:

_____ 1. We do have two different services which offer the small investor a discount from commission charge on regular way transactions. One of these, our Birdseye Plan, offers a rate that would be less than half that charged for a regular transaction of the size you describe. The other, a specialized Discount Plan, provides a 30% discount from the regular rates.

_____ 2. If your normal transaction is a very small one, we believe it would be to your advantage to avail yourself of one of these alternative plans. We suggest that you discuss these alternatives with your accountant, or Mr. Bob Barton.

_____ 3. Thank you for taking the time to write us of your concerns. We are most appreciative of your past patronage and trust that one of the plans will be suitable in achieving your objectives.

_____ 4. Very simply, our increase was designed to offset at least in part the cost increases we have experienced since 1985.

_____ 5. We realize no one welcomes higher prices. The fact is, though, that escalating costs in the last few years have caused most businesses to increase their prices. Indeed, it would be very difficult to single out any service that isn't higher priced now than it was a few years ago.

_____ 6. This is in further reply to your letter of June 30, 1985, directed to our President, Mr. Larry White.

Yours truly,

Exercise 19: SUBJECT/VERB AGREEMENT

Directions: Some, not all, of these sentences have grammatical errors. Circle the troublesome word(s) and rewrite the word(s) or sentence correctly.

1. Historical data and special instructions was not located.

2. Your twenty shares of stock was delivered to you.

3. There's several reasons for responding promptly to inquiries.

4. Which one of the employees are responsible for the error?

5. Revisions to the initial design are on the drawing board.

6. The locations assigned to Citizens and Southern Bank was converted to ACH.

Exercise 20: USING PARALLEL STRUCTURE IN A SENTENCE

Directions: Cross out the italicized, incorrect word(s) and write in the correct grammatical form. For example:

Incorrect: He thought about becoming a manager, clerk, or *selling*.
Correct: He thought about becoming a manager, clerk, or salesperson.

1. To write correctly is not necessarily *writing* effectively.

2. Early to bed and early to rise make a man healthy, wealthy, and *provides him with wisdom*.

3. We made these two suggestions—to increase sales and *for the education* of the individual customer.

4. I want to remind you of the office collection, which is now under way, and *urging you* to give your generous support.

Exercise 21: USING PARALLEL STRUCTURE IN LISTS

Directions: The following two examples came from a procedure manual and a weekly status report. Each item in the two lists begins with a different grammatical form. Change the italicized phrases so that each begins with a verb.

1. We request the following:
   a. *Printing on forms be more clear*
   b. *The attached listing be used for company abbreviations*
   c. *All pertinent information be included*
2. In our own department, we must:
   a. *Upgrade the basic functions of our clerks*
   b. *Our clerks must have their job functions clarified*
   c. *The importance of journal ID numbers must be stressed*

Rewrite:

Exercise 22: USING PARALLEL STRUCTURE IN PROCEDURAL MEMOS

Directions: The following descriptions of procedures are presented in typical sentence/paragraph format. Circle each verb or step in the procedure. On a separate sheet of paper rewrite each procedure by listing or bulleting all the steps.

MEMO 1

Subject: Procedure for Daily Time Cards

Each employee should figure his or her own time daily and keep a cumulative total on the upper right-hand side of the time card. This total should be *worked time only*—holidays, vacation, sick time, and so on should not be added into this cumulative total. All time *not worked but to be paid* (holidays, earned vacation/sick time, school, seminars, etc.) should be listed below the final cumulative total with the proper notation. Time should be calculated to the exact minute.

MEMO 2

Subject: Procedure for Daily Forms

On various occasions, data entry has not been able to read the information on these forms. We request that these forms be printed more legibly by your unit and that you use the listing we have developed for the company plan names. Attached are several copies for your use. In addition, please be sure all information is included on these forms: the office wire call, account number, etc.

☐ THE PRINCIPLES OF PERSUASION

Exercise 23: GETTING TO THE POINT

Directions: Read the following memo and then answer the questions below.

Subject: Chiller System

I would like to have our obsolete water chiller system, in the TA motor generator room, removed. These chillers and associated plumbing haven't been used for years and are taking up valuable floor space.

1. In the preceding memo, underline the word that tells the reader what *action* is expected.
2. Is this word buried or not?_____

3. Reorder the following questions according to the reader's interests: (a) What do I have to do? (b) Why should I do it? (c) Where do I have to go to do it?_____

4. Rewrite the opening sentence so the action word isn't buried.

Rewrite:

Exercise 24: ORDERING INFORMATION ACCORDING TO THE READER'S INTEREST

Directions: Pretend that you are a line manager and have just read a brochure announcing a Management Development Training Program. You are interested in sending some of your people to the program. The information presented in the brochure is described below. How would you want the information ordered? In the blanks provided, reorder the information according to what you consider critical information.

_____ **Programs Developed By:**
Training staff in the Human Resources Department, and designed to fit the expressed needs and experience of ABC supervisors.

_____ **Programs Presented By:**
Trainers in the Human Resources Department, and managers of Operations Areas' staff trainers certified to present each course.

_____ **Who Should Attend:**
First-line managers and supervisors of all Operations Areas. Also, experienced managers wanting to polish their skills.

_____ **Program Costs:**
No charge for course presented by the Human Resources Department staff in the home office.

_____ **How to Enroll:**
Contact the training staff of your Operations Area Personnel Department to obtain the appropriate enrollment card. Complete the card with your manager and return it to the Personnel Department for forwarding to the Human Resources Department.

Exercise 25: ORDERING ACHIEVEMENTS IN A RESUME

Directions: Read the following section from a resume and then answer the questions about it.

Special Achievements and Awards:

1. Jersey City State College
   Certificate for Academic Excellence, 1972–73
2. ABC Corporation Management Training
   Certificate of Achievement, 1974
3. Jersey City Minority Business Association
   Outstanding Young Businessman of the Year, 1975
4. XYZ Elementary School of Jersey City
   Member of the Board of Directors, 1976

Questions:

1. How is each achievement organized?
   Chronologically_____ According to the importance of the achievement _____
2. Within each numbered item, how is the information prioritized?
   Date _____ Institution _____ Award _____

3. Within each numbered item, how should the information be prioritized?

   Date _____ Institution _____ Award _____

4. Rewrite these achievements on a separate sheet of paper. First, reorder the information within each achievement. Second, prioritize the achievements from the most important to the least important.

Exercise 26: FRONTLOADING IN SUBJECT TITLES

Directions: Circle the power word and rewrite the subject title.

1. Subject: Escort Procedures Modification

2. Subject: Quality Teams Advanced Training

3. Subject: New York Facility Construction Bids

4. Subject: Late Mail Delivery Solution

5. Subject: October 1985 Status Report

6. Subject: Title Changes Procedure

Exercise 27: FRONTLOADING IN SENTENCES

Directions: Rewrite the following sentences and frontload the key phrases.

1. As a result of the new technology, our credit card numbers are changing.

2. On April 7, 1985, the Manager of Accounting and Reports, Steve Rachlis, confirmed that journal entries have not been approved.

3. We will coordinate with Data Entry to determine the required receipt time upon your approval of the attached list.

4. The quarterly statement will show a profit.

5. Based on discussed reporting requirements, Systems Development has undertaken an evaluation of time and manpower requirements.

6. Although a final decision has not been made yet, it does not appear that we will be able to accomplish the recapitalization.

7. On January 4, 1985, Mark D. Johnson, Director of Personnel, informed us that the aforementioned statements and acknowledgement forms are scheduled to be mailed during January.

8. As communicated to the Controller's Department, both unfamiliarity with the system and lack of time were the primary reasons for not transferring the current estimate.

Exercise 28: WRITING DYNAMIC SUBJECT TITLES

Directions: For the following examples, write subject titles that are interesting and tell the reader *something about* the subject.

1. Subject: Employee Benefits

2. Subject: Greybook Reporting

3. Subject: General Ledger System Automation

4. Subject: 1985 Sales Finance License

Exercise 29: USING REFERENCE HEADINGS

Directions: Rewrite the following opening paragraphs, using both a subject title and a reference heading (Re:).

1. Subject: _____

   Re: _____

   Per our phone conversation of 8/12, the branch office will close at 4 p.m. on Wednesday, November 21, for the Thanksgiving holiday.

2. Subject: _____

   Re: _____

   Pursuant to our phone conversations of Thursday, February 8, I want to put in writing the three main points we discussed as the highlights of our new sales promotions for January.

3. Subject: _____

   Re: _____

   June 27, 1985

   Dear Mrs. Parker,

   Please deposit the following municipal bearer bonds as discussed in the May 15 letter:
   1. $67,000 State of New Jersey Water
   2. $25,000 Housing Finance Corporation of the City of Newark, New Jersey

   This is for custodian account 556930 of the First National Bank of Sheboygan.

Exercise 30: BURYING "DISTRACTORS"

Directions: Rewrite the following sentences. Load the distracting words, "enclosed," "attached," or "reference," to the back of the sentence. Or, create a separate sentence for the distracting words.

1. Attached please find preliminary operating results for January.

2. Enclosed are Payment Request Forms for after-tax withdrawals.

3. The attached information provides an overview of participation under the Broadcasting Company Investment Plan.

4. Once this process is completed and with the approval of management (reference my August 29, 1985 memo), we would like to have permission to proceed.

Exercise 31: USING FOLLOW-UP STATEMENTS

Directions: The following sentences call for some degree of commitment to action. In the space provided, check the three sentences with the greatest commitment to action.

_____ 1. Please advise.

_____ 2. Let's discuss this.

_____ 3. Make an appointment to discuss this with me next week.

_____ 4. Call me on October 14.

_____ 5. I will call you on January 4 to make an appointment to discuss this with you.

_____ 6. Talk to you soon.

_____ 7. I will call you about this next week.

_____ 8. I am on your calender to review this plan for April 14 at 2:30.

☐ SELECTION OF EFFECTIVE WORDS

Exercise 32: REWRITING BUSINESS JARGON

Directions: The following sentences are examples of overused business language and of routine business tone. Rewrite the sentences, using fresher words.

1. As per our conversation today, the Quality Circle group will begin on Friday.

2. Pursuant to our agreement, invoices will be processed through Data Entry.

3. In accordance with your request, the disk drives will be delivered tomorrow.

4. Please be advised that as a result of the multitude of changes taking place at Sears, our credit card numbers are changing.

5. In response to your request, we will coordinate with Data Entry to determine your required receipt time.

6. We have been informed by Systems and Procedures that they are developing computer outputs.

7. Attached is the aforementioned memo from the Seattle office.

Exercise 33: REWRITING ROUTINE ENDINGS

Directions: Rewrite the following closings so that they are not vague, general, or "canned." Where possible, include specific information such as phone numbers, deadlines.

1. Thank you for your assistance.

2. If there are any problems, feel free to call me.

3. Thank you for your help regarding this situation.

Exercise 34: IMPRESSING VERSUS EXPRESSING

Directions: Read the following sentences out loud and give yourself the "WIST?" test (the "Would I Say That?" test). Change the formal words to words you might use in your natural speaking style.

1. Try to ascertain the facts.

2. The mail department procured two new stamp machines.

3. The aformentioned letter is attached.

4. I concur with your evaluation.

5. The said memo is damaging.

6. The annual report is forthcoming.

7. Your statement could have deleterious effects on the negotiations.

8. The rate per annum is 2%.

9. We can offer a quid pro quo of benefit to both client and organization.

10. This program is under our stewardship.

Exercise 35: USING WORDS THAT CREATE VISUAL IMAGES

Directions: In the space provided, check which of the two word choices creates the most action-oriented, interesting, and vivid image.

_____ 1. We *talked about* the new recommendations.
_____ We *discussed* the new recommendations.

_____ 2. Our team *sought out* the necessary resources.
_____ Our team *looked for* the necessary resources.

_____ 3. I *saw* progress in my unit.
_____ I *observed* progress in my unit.

_____ 4. The purpose of this memo is to *inform* you.
_____ The purpose of this memo is to *update* you.

_____ 5. I want your help in *stamping out* gobbledygook.
_____ I want your help in *eliminating* gobbledygook.

_____ 6. We need to *create* a new position.
_____ We need to *carve out* a new position.

_____ 7. The resources in our unit have been *inventoried.*
_____ The resources in our unit have been *accounted for.*

_____ 8. The purpose of the memo is to *map out* the new procedure.
_____ The purpose of this memo is to *outline* the new procedure.

☐ TONE AND STYLE

Exercise 36: IDENTIFYING THE PASSIVE AND ACTIVE VOICE

Directions: Place a "P" in front of passive sentences and an "A" in front of active ones.

_____ 1. Nelson Colon was transferred to the new department effective 3/18/85.

_____ 2. Nelson Colon transferred to the new department effective 3/18/85.

_____ 3. Each participant is given a copy of resources for effective writing.

_____ 4. The clerk is planning to expand operations on Tuesday.

_____ 5. Final procedures will be established by the task force.

_____ 6. The staff manager has been making a detailed audit.

_____ 7. By July the committee will have interviewed all applicants.

_____ 8. The rules were formulated by the president.

_____ 9. A farewell party has been planned in honor of the lead clerk.

_____ 10. Many customers are reached by direct mail.

Exercise 37: CHANGING THE PASSIVE VOICE TO ACTIVE VOICE

Directions: Change the following wordy and formal passive-voice sentences to active-voice sentences.

Passive: The information *has been received* by us.
Active: We *received* the information.

1. President Reagan's attempted assassination was filmed by a cameraman.

2. When Form 242 is received by us, the change will be made.

3. It was felt by both investigators that our questions would be answered by one phone call.

4. These proposals require that further data be furnished by Marketing.

5. Increased volume will affect the company if certain guidelines are not adhered to by this section.

6. The word-processing system was implemented on June 10, 1980, by this department.

7. The new forms will now be forwarded to Data Entry by your section.

8. Prior to the initiation of the new procedure, the change will be clarified by the manager.

9. The entire process on cash trades must be reevaluated by your department.

10. The customer should be informed by Marketing that CMA privileges have limits.

Exercise 38: CHANGING THE PASSIVE VOICE TO THE ACTIVE VOICE

Directions: Rewrite the following sentences, changing the passive voice to the active voice.

1. The CMA Customer Agreement was signed by you and gives ABC Company the right to cancel your CMA services.

2. Any present outstanding Visa charges presented for payment prior to the termination date will be honored provided there are sufficient funds in your account.

Exercise 39: RECYCLING NOUNS INTO VERBS

Directions: Find the hidden verb and recycle it from its noun form back into the verb form.

_____ 1. Take a look

_____ 2. Have intention

_____ 3. Offered a suggestion

_____ 4. Make substitution

_____ 5. Become an imposition

_____ 6. Made a proposal

_____ 7. Make a decision

_____ 8. Be of assistance

_____ 9. Take action

_____ 10. Give thought

Exercise 40: FINDING HIDDEN VERBS

Directions: Circle all "tion" endings and convert the words into verbs.

> *Example*: The policy's expira*tion* date is November 21.
> The policy *expires* on November 21.

1. This requires more of an explanation from you.

2. Your department's implementation of the plan was on 1/10/80.

3. These data need more organization on your part.

4. Would you please give consideration to this plan?

5. My co-worker offered the useful suggestion that we hire a time management team.

6. We request that you place one-hundred shares in segregation for this account.

7. Your lead clerk will receive instructions from me about the new procedure.

Exercise 41: CONVERTING NEGATIVE TONE TO POSITIVE TONE

Directions: These sentences are all real-life examples of business writing that have a negative tone. Circle the negative word(s) and rewrite the sentences so that you make the point in a positive way. For example:

Negative: To avoid further delay we will send this airmail . . .
Positive: So that you get this as soon as possible, we are sending . . .

1. No way will we be suckered into buying a second-class machine.

2. In the future, unless this is received in my department by 12:00 noon, we will no longer be willing to provide this service to you.

3. Paul Heim, our lead clerk, has performed well up to this point.

4. If you provide us with your information, we will be willing to share our information with you.

5. It is against our policy to let customers have regular checking accounts with balances under $500.

6. Unfortunately, the data are grossly inadequate.

7. This is an impossible situation to deal with.

Exercise 42: FINAL WRITING EXERCISE: REWRITING AN INEFFECTIVE LETTER

Directions: Rewrite the letter in Exercise 16 (page 189). Try to incorporate the principles of communication and persuasion by:

- Writing from the reader's viewpoint
- Frontloading the purpose
- Downplaying negative words
- Being concise
- Using persuasive messages
- Writing a more effective subject title

☐ ANSWER KEY

Exercise 1: IDENTIFYING PURPOSES OF WRITING

The one critical purpose is (1) to inform, (2) to create action, (3) to entertain, (4) to create action.

Exercise 2: CLARIFYING YOUR PURPOSE FOR WRITING

(1) I; (2) A; (3) I; (4) I,P; (5) P; (6) I,A; (7) P; (8) P; (9) I; (10) A

Exercise 3: IDENTIFYING PURPOSE STATEMENTS IN MEMOS

Memo 1: Purpose statement: Please approve credit of $355 to account 931-07899; we will charge account representative #4165.

Memo 2: Purpose statement: I am requesting your support and assistance to obtain the approvals required to begin . . .

Exercise 4: REWRITING PURPOSE STATEMENTS

The purpose of this proposal is to outline a management development program (or variations on this).

Exercise 5: USING VISUAL IMAGERY AS A CLARITY CHECK

Sentences 2 and 4 create clear pictures.

Exercise 6: INCLUDING A MISSING WORD

The missing word is "separate": Two *separate* time management classes . . .

Exercise 7: REPHRASING DISCONNECTED THOUGHTS

We are proud to have you as part of our team because you handle the callers with a professional and courteous attitude.

Exercise 8: SHORTENING LONG SENTENCES

1. I have two major "effective writing goals." They are to organize my thoughts logically and to capture my reader's attention.

2. Christy Levin has enhanced my unit immeasurably. She has an ability to produce under stress and still maintain the quality of her work. In addition, she takes suggestions in a constructive manner.

3. Three weeks ago a train bound for Manhattan from Queens broke down. It stranded 1,500 passengers in a tunnel under the East River for more than an hour. Concerned New York business people are banding together to lobby for change.

4. The dedication of the staff was above and beyond our expectations. It was the ingredient that allowed on-time completion of the project despite computer failures and the late delivery of materials.

5. Carrie Jones reported a minor problem in her section, which she assured me will be corrected promptly. This problem has no effect on our balancing procedure.

Exercise 9: BEING EXPLICIT

1. Please comment on your reactions to the four recommendations.

2. I would appreciate your speaking to the auditor by our deadline, August 14.

3. He averages forty-two trades a day as opposed to the company standard of fifty.

4. Call me at Ext. 9210 if you have any questions regarding July's income projections.

5. Productivity has increased 61 percent.

Exercise 10: BEING SPECIFIC

(1) 2,1,3; (2) 3,1,2; (3) 1,4,5,2,3; (4) 4,5,2,3,1

Exercise 11: COLUMNIZING NUMBERS

Stock	Number	Shares	Date	Comments
Exxon Corp.	26984	400	July 1986	• Columns do not crossfoot • No reconciliation
Louisville Gas & El.	89624	400	July 1986	• Columns do not crossfoot • No reconciliation received
NTL Corp.	52186	400	June 1986	• Code 6 rejected • Reconciliation received

Exercise 12: ELIMINATING REDUNDANT WORDS IN A SENTENCE

(1) "sincere" or "earnest," (2) "numerous" or "different," (3) "rules" or "regulations," (4) "ideas" or "concepts"

Exercise 13: SHORTENING WORDY EXPRESSIONS

(1) during; (2) for; (3) regarding, about, or for; (4) (use date); (5) if; (6) thanks; (7) regarding, about; (8) please; (9) please; (10) later, or give a date; (11) because; (12) in spite of, even though

Exercise 14: ELIMINATING UNNECESSARY WORDS IN A SENTENCE

1. Your check for $29.95 is enclosed., or Enclosed is your check for $29.95.
2. Please prepare the data because the transactions will take place.
3. Thank you for your April 20 receipt.
4. See Mr. Farren's attached memo about the accounting issues.
5. We promote talented people.
6. The annual budget for a finance corporation should answer two key questions: (a) What are management's desired objectives? (b) Are these objectives attainable?
7. Please write us by May 1.

Exercise 15: ELIMINATING "IT" EXPRESSIONS

1. I enjoyed meeting with you and Christy Levin last Monday.
2. I understand you will discuss this with Cynthia Lewis.
3. I have learned that some incoming phone calls are not being answered on a timely basis.
4. Please send us a new assessment of the property value.
5. ABC Company has paid the French withholding tax on the highest amount.
6. On Sunday you need to report early to power up all equipment.

Exercise 16: MAKING A WORDY LETTER CONCISE

Wordy	Concise
It is required by the Internal Revenue Service	The Internal Revenue Service requires
To assist us in this regard, we would appreciate it if you would kindly insert	Please insert
Thank you for your cooperation and assistance	Thank you for (choose one)

Exercise 17: ORGANIZING SENTENCES IN A LETTER

(1) 2; (2) 6; (3) 5; (4) 3; (5) 1; (6) 7; (7) 4

Exercise 18: ORGANIZING PARAGRAPHS

(1) 4; (2) 5; (3) 6; (4) 3; (5) 2; (6) 1

Exercise 19: SUBJECT/VERB AGREEMENT

1. Historical data and special instructions were not located.
2. Your twenty shares of stock were delivered to you.

3. There are several reasons for responding promptly to inquiries.
4. Which one of the employees is responsible for the error?
5. Correct as is.
6. The locations assigned to Citizens and Southern Bank were converted to ACH.

Exercise 20: USING PARALLEL STRUCTURE IN A SENTENCE

(1) to write; (2) wise; (3) to educate; (4) urge, or, to urge

Exercise 21: USING PARALLEL STRUCTURE IN LISTS

1. a. Print on forms clearly
   b. Use the attached listing for company abbreviations
   c. Include all pertinent information
2. a. Upgrade the basic functions of our clerks
   b. Clarify the job functions of our clerks
   c. Stress the importance of journal ID numbers

Exercise 22: USING PARALLEL STRUCTURE IN PROCEDURE MEMOS

MEMO 1

Subject: Time Cards

To fill out your time cards, please do the following daily:

1. Calculate all your times to the exact minute.
2. Add up your *actual worked time* (this does not include holidays, sick days, and vacation time).
3. Write down the cumulative total on the upper right-hand side of the time card.
4. Add up the time not worked but time paid for holidays, earned vacation/sick time, school, seminars, etc.
5. List this properly notated information below the final cumulative total.

MEMO 2

Subject: Daily Forms

On various occasions Data Entry has not been able to read the information on these forms. We request that you:

- Print more legibly
- Use the "Company Plan Names" listing (see attached copies)
- Include the following information:
    - Wire call number
    - Account number

Exercise 23: GETTING TO THE POINT

(1) removed; (2) yes; (3) a-1; b-3; c-2; (4) One possible rewrite is: Please remove the water chiller system from the TA motor generator room. This unused chiller is obsolete and is taking up valuable floor space.

Exercise 24: ORDERING INFORMATION ACCORDING TO THE READER'S INTEREST

These answers ultimately depend on your business situation. However, this would be a more persuasive order:

1. Who should attend
2. Cost (it's free—a benefit!)
3. Programs developed by *and* presented by you can be combined
4. How to enroll

The key in this exercise is that the writer erred by writing from his viewpoint. The reader's first concern is *not* who's presenting the program.

Exercise 25: ORDERING ACHIEVEMENTS IN A RESUME

1. Chronologically
2. Institution, award, date

3. Award, institution, date

4. a. Outstanding Young Businessman of the Year
   Jersey City Minority Business Association, 1975

   b. Board of Directors
   XYZ Elementary School of Jersey City, 1976

   c. Certificate of Achievement
   ABC Corporation Management Training, 1974

   d. Certificate for Academic Excellence
   Jersey City State College, 1972–73

Exercise 26: FRONTLOADING IN SUBJECT TITLES

Possible answers: (1) Modification for Escort Procedures; (2) Advanced Training for Quality Teams; (3) Construction Bids for New York Facility; (4) Solution for Late Mail Delivery; (5) Status Report for October 1985; (6) Procedure for Title Changes

Exercise 27: FRONTLOADING IN SENTENCES

1. Our credit card numbers are changing as a result of the new technology.

2. Journal entries currently have not been approved, as confirmed by Steve Rachlis, Manager of Accounting and Reports (4/7/85); or, Steve Rachlis, Manager of Accounting and Reports, confirmed that journal entries have not been approved (4/7/85).

3. Upon approval of the attached list, we will coordinate with Data Entry to determine your required receipt time.

4. A profit will be shown in the quarterly statement.

5. Systems Development has undertaken an evaluation of time and manpower requirements, based on discussed reporting requirements.

6. It does not appear that we will be able to accomplish the recapitalization, although a final decision has not been made yet.

7. The aforementioned statements and acknowledgment forms

are scheduled to be mailed during January, Mark D. Johnson, Director of Personnel, informed us on January 4, 1985.

8. The primary reasons for not transferring the current estimate were unfamiliarity with the system and lack of time, as communicated to the Controller's Department.

Exercise 28: WRITING DYNAMIC SUBJECT TITLES

Possible Answers: (1) Increase in Employee Benefits; (2) Request for Comments on Greybook Reporting; (3) Status of General Ledger System Automation; (4) Renewal of 1985 Sales Finance License

Exercise 29: USING REFERENCE HEADINGS

1. *Subject:* Closing time for Thanksgiving holiday
   Re: Our phone conversation of 8/12
2. *Subject:* New January sales promotions
   Re: Our phone conversations of February 8
3. *Subject:* Deposit of municipal bearer bonds
   Re: Letter of May 15, 1985

Exercise 30: BURYING "DISTRACTORS"

1. The preliminary operating results for January are attached.
2. The Payment Request Forms for after-tax withdrawals are enclosed.
3. An overview of participation under the Broadcasting Company Investment Plan is attached.
4. Once this process is completed and with the approval of management, we would like to have permission to proceed. (Please reference my August 29, 1985, memo.)

Exercise 31: USING FOLLOW-UP STATEMENTS

The statements with the most commitment are 5, 7, and 8, because the writer is taking responsibility for the next step and because a specific date or time is included. All the other statements are vague.

The date in 4 is not a commitment because it puts the responsibility on the reader.

Exercise 32: REWRITING BUSINESS JARGON

1. As we discussed today, the Quality Circle group will begin on Friday.
2. As we agreed, invoices will be processed through Data Entry.
3. Disk drives will be delivered tomorrow as you requested.

   or

   As you requested, disk drives will be delivered tomorrow.
4. As a result of the multitude of changes taking place at Sears, our credit card numbers are changing.
5. As you requested, we will coordinate with Data Entry to determine your required receipt time.
6. Systems and Procedures have informed us that they are developing computer outputs.
7. I am attaching the Seattle memo that I mentioned.

Exercise 33: REWRITING ROUTINE ENDINGS

Possible Answers:

1. Thank you for your assistance in seeing that the writing samples are handed in by the May 15th deadline.
2. If you find you are going to have any problems in delivering the furniture by our June 2nd deadline, please call me at Ext. 4721.
3. Thank you for your help in ensuring that the procedure for assessing the electronic mail system is followed.

Exercise 34: IMPRESSING VERSUS EXPRESSING

(1) find out; (2) purchased; (3) The letter I mentioned; (4) I agree; (5) this memo; (6) being sent August 10; (7) harmful; (8) per year; (9) mutual benefit; (10) sponsorship

Exercise 35: USING WORDS THAT CREATE VISUAL IMAGES

(1) discussed; (2) sought out; (3) observed; (4) update; (5) stamping out; (6) carve out; (7) inventoried; (8) map out

Exercise 36: IDENTIFYING THE PASSIVE AND ACTIVE VOICE

(1) P; (2) A; (3) P; (4) A; (5) P; (6) A; (7) A; (8) P; (9) P; (10) P

Exercise 37: CHANGING THE PASSIVE VOICE TO ACTIVE VOICE

1. A cameraman filmed President Reagan's attempted assassination.
2. When we receive Form 242 we will make the change.
3. Both investigators felt that one phone call would answer our questions.
4. These proposals require that Marketing furnish further data.
5. Increased volume will affect the company if this section does not adhere to certain guidelines.
6. This department implemented the word-processing program on June 10, 1980.
7. Your section will forward the new forms to Data Entry.
8. The manager will clarify the change prior to the initiation of the new procedure.
9. Your department must reevaluate the entire process on cash trades.
10. Marketing should inform the customer that CMA privileges have limits.

Exercise 38: CHANGING THE PASSIVE VOICE TO THE ACTIVE VOICE

1. You signed the CMA Customer Agreement which gives ABC Company the right to cancel your CMA service.
2. We will honor any present outstanding Visa charges pre-

sented for payment prior to the termination date provided there are sufficient funds in your account.

Exercise 39: RECYCLING NOUNS INTO VERBS

(1) look; (2) intend; (3) suggest; (4) substitute; (5) impose; (6) proposed; (7) decide; (8) assist; (9) act; (10) think

Exercise 40: FINDING HIDDEN VERBS

1. Please explain this further.
2. Your department implemented the plan on 1/10/80.
3. Please organize the data.
4. Please consider this plan.
5. My co-worker suggested that we hire a time management team.
6. We request that you segregate one-hundred shares for this account.
7. I will instruct your lead clerk about the new procedure.

Exercise 41: CONVERTING NEGATIVE TONE TO POSITIVE TONE

1. We will purchase only a first-class machine.
2. We will be able to continue providing this service to you if this is received in my department by 12:00 noon.
3. Paul Heim, our lead clerk, has performed well.
4. We would like to trade information with you.
5. You can have a regular checking account with a minimum balance of $500.
6. We need fifty percent more data with one-hundred percent accuracy.
7. This is an extremely difficult situation to deal with.

Exercise 42: REWRITING AN INEFFECTIVE LETTER

The following is one possible way to rewrite the letter. The exact wording will differ from person to person. The critical point is not so much the wording but that:

- The letter be written from the reader's viewpoint
- The purpose be upfront
- "IRS" and red flag language not be frontloaded
- Unnecessary language be omitted
- An action statement and accessibility statement be included

Up front purpose

Subject: (Request) for Tax Information

Dear Ms. Sweetnam: *Specific action*

(Please write) your tax identification number in the space provided below. By identification number we mean either a social security number if you are an individual or an identification number if you are an employer.

We need this tax information for Form 1099 for the 1985 tax year.

Please return this letter in the envelope we have provided. If you have any questions regarding our request, please call (744-9192). Thank you for your help in meeting our January 24th (deadline.)

deadline   *accessibility statement*

Note that the information is ordered according to the reader's questions:

Paragraph 1: *Why* are you writing to me?
              What do I have to DO?
Paragraph 2: *Why* do I have to do it?
Paragraph 3: *How* do I proceed?

9

Resources on Writing

This chapter discusses resources you can use to train yourself to write after reading this book. It includes:

- A detailed checklist on the principles of communication and persuasion.
- A summary of the key points in each chapter.
- A checklist on what to include in memos.
- A checklist on measuring your growth in writing.
- Models for:
  - Information memos,
  - Letters of apology,
  - Proposals,
  - Sales letters,
  - Tough messages.
- A reading list.

□ CHECKLIST ON THE PRINCIPLES OF COMMUNICATION

_____ 1. *Use your wisdom as a reader.*
- Make your writing easy to read.
- Make it brief.

_____ 2. *Clarify your writing goals.*
- Establish your critical purpose for writing:
  - to inform,
  - to persuade,
  - to create action.
- Place purpose statements up front.

_____ 3. *Be brief.*
Strive for the "one page policy."

_____ 4. *Be clear.*
- Be explicit so there's no room for misinterpretation.
- Tend toward short sentences.
- Follow the rule: one idea per sentence.
- Be specific.
- To test for clarity conduct these two tests:
  - TV Show Test,
  - HWIST (How Would I Say This?) Test.

_____ 5. *Be concise.*
- Avoid redundancy.
- Shorten wordy phrases.
- Avoid vague "it" and "there" expressions.
- Place many numbers in columns.

_____ 6. *Be complete.*
- Make sure your communication has three sections:
  - introduction,
  - body,
  - closing.

> • Use headings for multiple readers.
> • Give the "So what?" test to everything you write.

_____ 7. *Be correct.*
> • Check for subject/verb agreement.
> • Use parallel grammatical structure.

_____ 8. *Make your presentation attractive.*
> • Use "block left" formatting.
> • Tend towards short paragraphs.
> • Use highlighting techniques:
>   · white space,
>   · headings,
>   · bullets.

☐ CHECKLIST ON THE PRINCIPLES OF PERSUASIVE WRITING

_____ 1. *Write from the reader's viewpoint.*
> • Consider ordering information psychologically rather than automatically writing chronologically.
> • Use reader logic when you order sentences.
> • Use pronouns "you" and "your."

_____ 2. *Get to the point!*
> • State your main point up front:
>   · in the subject title,
>   · in paragraphs,
>   · in sentences.
> • Try using reference headings.

_____ 3. *Position your ideas.*
> • Write for your reader's memory:
>   · your first paragraph holds the most power—the middle section may or may not get read.

- Avoid putting key points in no-man's land (the bottom one third of the page).

_____ 4. *Use the three messages of persuasion:*
  - Purpose statements.
  - Benefit statements.
  - Follow-up statements.

☐ SUMMARY OF THE CHAPTERS

Style

General Comments
- Develop a range of styles.
- The person with the clout decides what communication style to use.
- Maintain a constant style with each person.

Strategies for Being Forceful
- Use short sentences.
- Emphasize verbs.
- Recycle nouns into verbs.
- Minimize use of the passive voice.

Strategies for Being Personal
- Use pronouns.
- Avoid using the distancing word "one."

Strategies for Being Interesting
- Be yourself.
- Write like you speak.

Words

- Select specific words rather than general ones.
- Use words that create mental images.
- Avoid overly casual language.
- Use words the reader is familiar with.
- Try to avoid negative words.

Tone

- Use positive tone.
- Try to turn negatives into positives.

Getting Started

- Start writing about what you know best.
  - Try using these strategies for getting started:
  - Write down thoughts while they're fresh in your mind.
  - Use the Jean Bubley dialogue method.
  - Write a purpose statement: "The purpose of writing this memo is to. . . ."
- Try mindmapping.
- Try freewriting.

The Process of Writing

- Start writing sooner.
- Take one step at a time:
  1. Think
  2. Plan
  3. Write
  4. Edit

Recognize How You Inhibit Your Writing Ability

- You procrastinate.
- You edit in your head, not on paper.
- You criticize yourself as you write.
- Beware of the physical signs of self-criticism:
    - Erasing.
    - Crossing out words.
    - Throwing away your paper.
    - Going to the dictionary and thesaurus.
    - Stopping for spelling and punctuation.
    - Constantly rereading.

How to Give Your Memo a Test Run

- Read out loud what you've written.
- Set up a formal "editing buddy system."
- Use good secretaries.
- Proofread your work before you send it.

How to Have More Effective Editing Sessions with Others

- Avoid the trap of debating about "good" writing.
- Insist on specific editorial comments.
- Ask specific questions about your writing.
- Stand up for the points you are committed to.
- Don't argue over trivia.

Managing Your Time and Space

- Set priorities.
- Write during your "prime time."
- Write in chunks of time.

- Write when you can concentrate.
- Write in privacy.

How to Keep Writing in Perspective

- Each memo is a grain of sand in the whole scheme of things.
- "The paper you" is not the real you.
- Compare yourself only with yourself.

☐ MEMO CHECKLIST

These are principles to check for when you're writing in business:

Principles of Communications

_____ Make it short and easy to read.

_____ Clarify your goals.

_____ Be brief.

_____ Be clear.

_____ Be concise.

_____ Be complete.

_____ Organize your ideas.

_____ Be correct.

_____ Make your presentation attractive.

Principles of Persuasion

_____ Write from the reader's viewpoint.

_____ Get to the point.

_____ Position your ideas.

_____ Use the three messages of persuasion:

      _____ Purpose statements.
      _____ Benefit statements.
      _____ Follow-up statements.

_____ Tend toward short sentence and paragraph length.

_____ Use highlighting techniques:

      _____ Bullets.
      _____ Headings.
      _____ White space.

☐ CHECKLIST FOR MEASURING YOUR GROWTH IN WRITING

You can measure your progress by observing certain proofs:

_____ 1. **You Get Quicker Responses from Your Readers:** If the normal turn-around time on a request memo is two weeks, and you get a response in two days, you know you are communicating more effectively with your reader.

_____ 2. **You Receive Inner Satisfaction from What You Have Written:** You know when you have written something good because you have a feeling of "rightness" about it. You are more willing to "let go" of good writing with both your typist and your reader.

_____ 3. **You Enjoy Writing More:** If you find that you fear a blank piece of paper less, and can tackle a writing task with less procrastination, you are gaining self-confidence in your writing skills.

_____ 4. **You Receive Positive Feedback:** When you get a compliment on a well-written letter, or your co-workers ask for your editing advice, you know that those around you respect your ability to write effectively.

☐ MODELS FOR WRITING

The following are models you can use as a plan for your written communications. They are one option for _what_ messages to include and _how to order_ those messages.

Information Memos
Purpose
Problem
Solution
Follow-up

Model for a Letter of Apology
Reference message
Good-news message
Apology/empathy message
Documentation message
Goodwill message

Model for a Proposal

Hello
Background
Problem
Solution
Benefits of the solution
Implementation:
· Steps
· Dates
Follow-up

Sales Letters

Purpose statement
Problem or need statement (optional)
Benefit statements
Follow-up statements

Tough-Message Letter

KISS
KICK
KISS

☐ A READING LIST

Writing Tips from Successful Advertisers

Ken Roman and Joel Raphaelson, *Writing That Works*, Harper and Row, New York, 1981.

Comprehensive and Excellent Reading

David W. Ewing, *Writing for Results in Business, Government, the Sciences and the Professions*, Wiley, New York 1979.

Excellent Article on Business Style

John S. Fielden, "What Do You Mean, You Don't Like My Style?," *Harvard Business Review*, May–June (1982).

Brief, Clear Reference Book on Correct English

W. Strunk and E.B. White, *Elements of Style*, MacMillan, New York, 1979.

Freewriting

Gabriele Lusser Rico, *Writing the Natural Way*, J.P. Tarcher, distributed by Houghton Mifflin, New York, 1983.

Managing Your Writing Time

Alan Lakein, *How to Get Control of Your Time and Your Life*, Signet, New York, 1973.

Gaining Confidence in Your Writing

Brenda Ueland, *If You Want to Write*, The Schubert Club, St. Paul, MN, 1983.

Index